"Power moves to those who are truly committed to serving."
Anthony Robbins

# Chapter 1

"Platinum."

"Pardon me? I don't think I heard you right."

The jeweler chuckled softly. "I said it's platinum, young fellow. And you are...?"

The young man immediately stuck his hand out. "Aaron."

The jeweler nodded as he shook Aaron's hand. "My name is Bob. Good to meet you Aaron. I was saying that this business card you have here is made of platinum. Except the logo, which is gold."

Aaron looked surprised but remained silent, trying to process what he was hearing. Finally he spoke up again. "Are you absolutely certain Bob? I mean, can you really tell just by looking at it? I would have thought that you might have to examine it or something..."

Bob smiled. "You mean you *assumed* I might need to do some sort of examination? Not thought...assumed?"

Aaron nodded. "Yes, you're right. I assumed. But...how do you know the card is platinum from just a glance, if you don't mind me asking?"

"I know because I made these cards. A gentleman approached me a few years ago with the design and requested that I make them. What was the name of the man who gave you this card?" Bob asked.

Aaron shared his story. "His name is Steve. He came into my store the other day and over the course of about an hour, I helped him decide on some purchases. Steve left the store, but then came back a few minutes later. He said he was really impressed with my service. Then he tucked his business card into my shirt pocket. I was busy with some other customers, but I took a minute to talk to him. Steve said that if I was ever interested in making a lot more money than I am now, to come and find him."

Aaron paused, recalling his unusual customer.

"It wasn't until later that I had a chance to look at the card. All it had on it was the logo, quotation, and an address on the back of it. Not your average looking business card, so I came to find him at the listed address, which turned out to be your jewellery store. Now you're telling me that the card is made of platinum...? To be honest, I'm not really sure what to do next."

Bob the jeweler nodded as Aaron came to the end of his story. "That sounds like Steve alright. And I can help you figure out what to do next. Steve gave you that card to bring you here. Now that you're here it's my job to offer you a couple of choices. One is easy, one is difficult. Are you ready to hear them?"

Aaron nodded, not really sure what to expect, but more curious than ever.

Bob stood a bit taller and his bearing became more formal, almost as if he was standing up to talk in front of a crowd. He held the platinum business card out to Aaron, who took it.

"Aaron, my new friend, please read the inscription beneath the apple on the front of the card."

Aaron looked at the card and studied its features for perhaps the hundredth time. It was a heavy, metallic business card with very little information on it. In the middle of the card was the imprint of a perfect-looking golden apple, with a spear-shaped leaf hanging from the stem. Beneath the imprint of the apple was a sentence which Aaron now read aloud: "If one bad apple can spoil the bunch ...What can a gold apple do?"

Bob nodded, smiling. "Thanks, Aaron. I still get a warm tingle when I hear that question. Okay, here are your two choices. Number one: you can turn in this card and I will give you its cash value. Then you walk out of here and we likely never see each other again. This is the easy choice, and the one that I suggest you take."

"Or...choice number two: you can trade this card for another card. The new card will have another address on the back. You can either go to that address, or choose to do nothing. If you accept this new card you get no money, and forfeit the reward offered for the platinum card. This is the tough choice. Both are simple, and before you leave here today you must decide on Option 1 or 2. Do you have any questions before you decide?"

"Yeah, I have a big question! If I turn the card in how much money will I get?"

Bob smiled. "$10,000."

Aaron's eyes widened. $10,000 was a lot of money. There must be a catch.

"Why offer me so much money? I don't get it."

Bob shook his head. "It's a legitimate offer Aaron. There's no catch. Steve is a customer service fanatic and he sometimes tips people who give him excellent, outstanding service. Your tip is the card, and the card is redeemable for $10,000.00. It's his card and his rules."

"So...what's the next address? Will that take me to Steve?"

"It takes you *towards* Steve. I haven't heard of him showing up so quickly though, so my bet would be you won't see him there. But it takes you in the right direction."

Aaron hesitated. "I gotta tell you Bob, this is sounding a bit weird. A little dangerous, actually. I've never been in this type of situation and, I must admit, I'm a little concerned. I sure don't want to end up dead and stuffed in a dumpster bin somewhere."

Bob looked at Aaron solemnly. "Aaron, I can tell you that you'll never be in any type of danger. This isn't a game, it's a journey. Steve would never harm a soul. Trust me, you'll be fine."

"How long will this journey take?"

"There's no specific time frame, Aaron. It could take a few weeks, or it can take a lifetime. But each step is up to you. It's always up to you."

"Okay Bob, I have one more question, and then I'll make my decision. Has anyone ever taken this worthless paper card and made more than $10,000 as a result?"

Bob reached below the counter and drew a new card with the same logo and phrase as the platinum card. It appeared to be made of regular card stock but was gold in colour. As he set it on the counter, Bob smiled and looked Aaron in the eye.

"Yes Aaron, the paper card has turned into more than $10,000 for others. And the ones who have made the truly large sums of money always asked me the same question you just did. Now.... it's time to choose."

Aaron thought for a moment, took a deep breath, and chose.

# Chapter 2

"Ross will only be another minute or two. He has one issue in the kitchen and then he'll be right out."

Aaron smiled and thanked the hostess.

An internet search had led him to the address on the second golden apple card. He stood at the entrance of a restaurant named 'Customer's Paradise'. It was THE restaurant in town. If you wanted to eat there then you made a reservation, and you made it at least eight months in advance. The prices were reasonable, the food was excellent, and the service was incredible.

Aaron looked at the menu while he waited. On the bottom corner of the front cover was a small picture of a gold apple—the same gold apple that appeared on the card in Aaron's pocket. This must be the right place, thought Aaron.

A sharply dressed man approached him. He was about six feet tall, with a friendly, confident smile.

"Hi I'm Ross. How can I help you ......?" The way he left the sentence hanging left room for really only one response.

Aaron introduced himself and shook Ross's hand.

Ross smiled and said, "Aaron! Great to meet you! Always good to meet someone for the first time! You have either not eaten here before, or I don't remember you. And if I don't remember you then I might be ready to retire. So please help me keep my job and tell me truthfully, which is it?"

"Don't worry Ross you're not losing your memory." Aaron said, liking this guy instantly. "I haven't had a chance to eat here yet. Would you really remember me if I had?"

"Absolutely," said Ross. "If I don't greet a customer by name on sight, then I will close the doors immediately."

Aaron was intrigued. "Wow that's pretty risky. If you have a bad day or get distracted, you'll close down a hugely successful business simply because of a forgotten name?"

Ross shook his head. "It might seem like a small thing, forgetting someone's name...but in this restaurant it's actually breaking a very important rule, our first rule of customer service. If I consider it acceptable to break that rule ...... well then, eventually I will break it. Once I start doing things like that, our customers will slowly stop coming back, and we will suffer the same fate as so many restaurants that didn't take care of their clientele. To prevent this from happening, I have a strict rule. If I forget a customer's name that I've already met......I will close the restaurant immediately. Every day that we're open is a day that we appreciate and remember our customers sincerely."

His serious look melted into that friendly smile again. "But I'm rambling. How can I help you today?"

Aaron fished the card out of his pocket. "I got this card from a guy named Bob, and the address written on the back is yours. I was hoping that it might lead me to another gentleman who goes by the name of Steve. Is he available?"

"I should have guessed it!" Ross exclaimed, laughing out loud. "You pulled me into a tutorial on the first rule of service so easily, so naturally, I should have guessed it!"

"Guessed what?" asked Aaron. "I'm afraid I don't understand."

"That's okay, Aaron. I'm just laughing at myself. Come on back to my office for a bit and I'll try to explain some things for you."

Aaron nodded, ready to follow. "That would be much appreciated."

On the way to Ross's office they walked through the dining room and Aaron noticed something interesting. Every table was full. Aaron had come to the restaurant at 3:00 p.m., which was usually a slow time between the lunch rush and the dinner crowd. This wasn't the case here though. Almost every table was occupied. Waiters and waitresses moved in an unhurried yet purposeful pace throughout the restaurant. Each staff member was smiling comfortably, appearing relaxed and confident even though they were busy. The same type of calm assuredness could be seen in the kitchen staff as Aaron and Ross moved past the immaculate grill and cooking area. Aaron had worked in restaurants before and he could tell that this one was different in many ways.

Ross's office looked similar to most, but there was one big difference. The desk was pushed directly against the wall and two chairs were positioned side by side, instead of being across from each other. Ross sat down in one seat and motioned for Aaron to take the other.

"So have you ever worked in a restaurant before Aaron?"

Aaron nodded affirmatively. "Yes I have. I started off washing dishes in a nice little restaurant back in my hometown. After doing that for a summer, I moved into a part time cook position and worked weekends and after school. Once I was old enough, I followed the money and moved out to the front of the house to become a waiter."

Ross nodded. "You did look comfortable walking through this place. Do you still work in the restaurant business?"

"No, at the moment I'm helping a friend get his business off the ground. He felt I would be able to help him succeed in his new venture. It was a challenge and the money was good, so I figured I'd give it a try."

Ross leaned back a bit in his seat, naturally matching Aaron's posture. "So you were moving nicely through life helping build your friend's business when, out of nowhere, Steve came and threw a wrench into things? That sounds just like him. If you don't mind me asking, Aaron, this card in your hand now ... Is it the first one he gave to you?"

Aaron shook his head. "No, he gave me a card made of platinum. I exchanged it for this one from Bob, the jeweler."

The smile on Ross's face froze for a brief second, and then he leaned forward and let out a slow whistle. "A platinum apple card, well now, that changes things quite a bit. Coming here with that gold apple card in your hand means you get a job here, if you want one. But if you were given a platinum apple card then you have other options as well."

It was Aaron's turn to smile. "You would offer me a job just because I came here with this gold apple card?"

Ross nodded. "Absolutely, anyone with a gold apple card is worthy of a job here. Actually that's the only way to get a job at Customer's Paradise. We're way much too successful and busy to accept strangers. We need people who excel at providing great customer service. Bringing the card in tells me that you possess the qualities, which are rare to find and can't be trained easily. The only question I would have for you is what position do you want?"

Aaron laughed. "What job do I want? "But what if I have no experience?" Or what if I told you I was a cook but had experience only as a dishwasher?"

"Then I would train you to do the job you wanted. And from long experience in this business, since you're the bearer of that card, you'd excel at the training and become a great cook and team member here." Ross paused for a second. "If you were a dishwasher would you come to me and claim that you were a cook?"

"No, I wouldn't lie about something like that."

Ross nodded. "That's one of the reasons you hold a gold apple card, you wouldn't lie about something important. If you really were a dishwasher and wanted to try your hand at cooking, then you would be honest and ask for a chance to be a cook." Aaron nodded in agreement.

"Has anyone told you what the gold apple card represents?" Ross asked.

Aaron shook his head slowly. "No, no one has told me much of anything at all. I've been to the jeweler's, and then here." With a sly grin Aaron continued. "So far I've turned down $10,000 and been offered a job as a cook."

Ross let out a big laugh and reached into his drawer, pulling out a small box. Inside the box were about 30 or 40 gold apple cards, identical to Aaron's.

"Ok Aaron, Here's what the gold apple card signifies. Possessing the gold apple card means that you have a natural ability to deliver extraordinary and excellent customer service. I believe that this ability is the single most important factor for attaining success. If you look closely at any successful person, regardless of what they tell you they do for a living, they are all naturals at delivering great customer service.

Ross paused. Aaron didn't look too impressed at hearing this revelation, but Ross was used to such a reaction. No one gave much credit to the power of excellent customer service.

Ross smiled confidently and continued his explanation. "Aaron, this is one of the best restaurants in the world. I'm not bragging out of hand, everyone agrees. There is one reason for our incredible reputation and one reason only: we consistently provide our customers with extraordinary customer service. Every single person here excels at delivering superb customer service, and each one of them got their job by walking up to me and handing me a gold apple card. We train the basic mechanics of the job, but each person here brings their special gift to give impeccable customer service in everything they do. You bring me a card; you can have a job here. You take a job here and you make more money than any other person working the same position in any other restaurant around, guaranteed. Every employee here wins, which allows our customers to benefit most of all."

Aaron let this information sink in, and then considered it aloud. "Excellent customer service, I understand. But what else is required to get the gold apple card? There must be more to it than that."

Ross shook his head. "No, there is not more to it. The ability to provide extraordinary customer service is all that's required. That's because nothing else is as important. True customer service is so rare that it can turn anything to gold. It's the secret key to success in everything. If you're able to give spectacular customer service then you're rare, and you can excel above all others. It's kind of funny that being good at helping others can lead to such success, but it can."

Aaron couldn't believe what he was hearing. "This doesn't make sense, how could something that simple be so important? It's easy to do. Everyone can do it if they just think a bit and apply themselves."

Ross chuckled. "You say that only because to you, it's easy. Common sense is not as common as you might think. Let me ask you a question. How good are you at writing music?"

"I'm terrible at it." Aaron replied. "There's no way I could ever write a song or music. I'm always amazed that they can put words to music, it's like magic as far as I'm concerned."

Ross nodded. "That sounds just like me. With a gun to my head I could not compose a tune. But when I ask a songwriter how they do it, they just shrug and say that it's easy for them. They just hear the music and write it down. Often a good songwriter will say that writing a song is just common sense. You see Aaron, providing excellent customer service is common sense to those who have the natural ability. To the rest of the world it might as well be magic. If you're still not convinced, then quickly give me five examples of excellent customer service you have received today."

Aaron opened his mouth, but Ross interrupted him. "Examples that don't involve this restaurant."

Aaron's mouth quickly closed. After about 30 seconds of thinking he said, "To be honest, I can't think of one. If I even travel a week into the past I can only think of maybe one. That's not good."

"No." Ross sighed. "That's not good at all. It's a shame, really. We live in a time when, to most people, 'customer service' is just two words in a phrase. Hundreds of thousands of people are given the job of customer service, yet almost none of them have any idea how to do it. Just like everything really, there are always more jobs than qualified people to fill them." Ross's frown turned into a smile. "But that's good news for us Aaron. It makes those of us who give good customer service popular people. We can also support and not be jealous of each other. The opportunities for us are unlimited, so it's not as if we're all applying for the same job. If the world suddenly discovered a million Gold Apples there would still be room for millions more."

"So you're saying that customer service isn't everything, it's the only thing?"

Ross nodded. "That's exactly what I'm saying. You name a product, business, or characteristic that you believe is better than customer service. I'll prove to you that your example actually is customer service. Many have tried to best me in this, and they usually fail. That's why I'm your first exposure to the Gold Apples, because I see it so clearly. I'm a customer service freak, and as a result, I'm very successful."

Aaron nodded his head in understanding. "Well I'm flattered that you're offering me a job Ross, thank you. Normally I'd consider it, but lately being an employee is starting to get boring. Maybe now is the time for me to start a business of my own. For years my customer service has earned my employers big sums of money. I think that now is the time to make the transition from employee to business owner and start to make some serious cash for myself."

Ross smiled, "That's the spirit, Aaron. The world can never have too many good businesses." He reached into another drawer and pulled out a different gold apple card. "Because you were given the platinum Gold apple card you get two other things from me. The first one is this card. It has another address on the back of it, for your next visit if you continue your journey. The second one is an explanation of the first rule of customer service." Ross paused with the new card held out towards Aaron. "Would you like to reconsider my job offer? I think you'd learn a great deal here and have a great time. Who knows, maybe in a couple years a franchise opportunity will open up......?"

Aaron reached out and accepted the new card, examining the back and finding another address written there. "Once again, thanks for the offer, but I'm going to pass. I think it would be fun to work here. Everyone looks like they're having a great time. No one appears upset or stressed and I bet there are a lot of tips to be made. This card quest has me intrigued though; I think I'll take my next clue and move towards finding Steve."

"OK." said Ross. "Then let me tell you about the first rule of customer service. The First Rule of Customer Service is this: Always answer your customer's primary unspoken question....Do You Care About Me?"

"I have an analogy to share with you that helps illustrate this rule. Let's say you're checking in for your flight at the airport. There is a lady helping you at the ticket counter. After she puts your info into the computer she looks up and says, 'I'm sorry, Sir, but it looks like this flight is totally booked up and there isn't a seat available for you." She then stares patiently at you, saying nothing. Quick! What are you thinking?"

Aaron thought for a second. "Well, I'm not too pleased. I've booked a flight and now I'm standing at the airport ready to go, only to be told that I have no plane to get on. I'm thinking 'what am I supposed to do now?'"

Ross nodded. "That sounds about right. And how do you feel about the girl at the counter just looking at you?"

"To say it politely, I'm frustrated with her at the moment." Aaron said. "She seems to be able to give me the bad news, but I need help and she's just standing there offering me nothing. I will ask her what my options are even though I'm already a little upset that I have to ask such an obvious question."

"Okay, Aaron. Now to continue with my example, let's say that you do ask her what your options are. The girl looks back down at her computer screen and types away for 20 seconds or so. Then she looks up and replies, "Sir, I have no idea what your options are. The flight is full. There is nothing that I can do, I'm sorry." Then the same patient stare. How do you feel now?"

Aaron shook his head agitatedly. "I'm angry is how I feel. I'm mostly angry because the ticket girl has ruined my day and doesn't even seem to care about it."

"Perfect!" Ross exclaimed, laughing as he did so. "I couldn't have said it any better. And you have just illustrated the first rule of customer service, the negative aspect of it, anyway. The girl at the ticket counter answered a very important question for you: 'Do you care about me?' When the answer to this question is 'no', then it's impossible to feel that you have received good customer service. Do you agree?"

"I completely agree with you, Ross. I realize things happen in life that can't be controlled. Having no airplane seat would've been unexpected and a cause for some concern, but it's not the end of the world. The absolute worst part of the scenario you described is that I don't know what to do and no one wants to help me."

Ross nodded sympathetically. "You're right. Now let me give you the same story but with a different ending."

"You're checking in for your flight at the airport. There's a lady helping you at the ticket counter. After she puts your info into the computer she looks up and says, "Sir, I'm seeing a slight problem with the flight, but I'm certain we can fix it and get you quickly in the air and towards your destination. The flight has been over-booked and, through no fault of yours, there is not a seat available for you. Even though it's rare, I've seen this happen before and here is how we normally fix it. You can wait for the next plane, which boards about 25 minutes after this one and only a couple of gates away so the walk is not too bad. Actually that's the best option I have at the moment, Sir. We would be happy to buy you a snack at the café beside your new gate if you would like? I realize that puts you behind by a half hour or so and sometimes that's not good. Will this cause you to be late for anything or does it sound acceptable?'" Ross seemed to enjoy playing the part of an excellent customer service provider. With a smile, he turned to Aaron.

"So tell me, does this sound any different from the first example?"

Aaron didn't hesitate. "It sounds much, much better. She offered me a solution, and then asked if the half hour would be a bad thing for me. She totally cared about my problem and wanted to help me solve it."

Ross shook his head slightly. "She didn't only care about your problem...she cared about *you*. And because she did, your problem became her problem. I've experienced service of both types many times over the years. I think that we all have. I can't tell you the names of all the incorrectly titled 'customer service' people like the first lady that I've encountered. I can, however, tell you the name of the second lady I described. Her name was Lynn and she helped me out of a similar situation. I wish it had been as simple as I described in the example. Lynn actually put me on a speeding 40-minute cab ride to a nearby airport so I could catch a plane and get to my destination on time...all at no cost to me! Most people would have let me wait six hours for the next flight from the first airport, but Lynn cared about me and looked for a better solution to get me in the air as quickly as possible. I will always remember her, and because of her I'm a loyal customer of the airline she represents." Ross paused, and then asked. "You're a loyal customer also? Do you have businesses that you go back to over and over again?"

Aaron smiled. "Yes, when I get great service I go back again and again. I get my hair cut in a city an hour away from my current home, because I get a great cut there and from day one they've been excellent with their service. I like it when customers appreciate my service and come back to me, so I try to do the same thing."

Ross chuckled. "You're a Gold Apple alright. No matter how many times I meet one, I get a kick out of seeing the same or very similar qualities in us. The young Gold Apples think I'm a wizard because I can accurately identify some of their personality traits. Really it's just experience from seeing the same characteristics in people who are so alike."

"Have you met many platinum card holders?" asked Aaron. "Do they have common traits also?"

"I've seen a few platinums. Let me ask you a couple questions and see how my magic works. You have an excellent memory when it comes to events and people?"

Aaron nodded.

"If I asked you how many self help books you've read, tapes you've listened to, and seminars you've attended... you could give me at least five titles off the top of your head—complete with the author or speaker?"

Aaron laughed out loud. "Yes I could easily give you 5!"

"In almost every job or activity you participate in, you're a leader who others naturally tend to follow. You're not brazen or loudmouthed, and I'm not saying you're the best at most things, but over a short period of time, others begin to ask you for your opinions...your help...and you just start to instinctively train and teach?"

"Bingo," replied Aaron shaking his head in wonder.

"You constantly come up with ideas. Every time you see a challenge you can come up with multiple strategies for reaching a solution?"

Aaron just smiled.

"I'll take that as a yes. You ask lots of questions? Not only do you ask lots of questions but you spend most conversations listening to other people talk about their experiences instead of 'boring' others with your uneventful life and details?"

"Wow," said Aaron, amazed. "It's like you spend most of your days following me around. That's me pretty much to a tee."

Ross nodded. "People come in types. Some of those types see patterns wherever they look. If you can see patterns, then it's easy to identify different groups and their strengths and qualities. But you know that, don't you Aaron? You're platinum, so you likely also possess this ability to see patterns?"

Aaron nodded. "Yes I do notice patterns. Thanks Ross, I appreciated that demonstration."

"It was my pleasure. Now back to the First Rule of Customer Service. Do you have any questions about what I've said?"

Aaron shifted forward in his chair. "Answer the unspoken question: 'Do you care about me?' It's simple and makes clear sense to me, Ross. I'm positive that I do this when I'm working and dealing with people, but before you explained it I wouldn't have guessed that it would be the first rule of anything. Now that I think about it, though, showing people that you care about them really is a key factor for giving great service."

Ross stood up and walked towards the door. "If you did nothing else but followed the first rule, you would give extraordinary customer service. That's what makes it number one in our books. Every Gold Apple instinctively applies the first rule. Every employee in this restaurant cares about each customer they encounter. The customers feel our concern for them, and they reward us by coming back again and again. A great win-win situation. You admitted earlier that the average person gets almost no good service in a regular day. When they come to a place where they get exceptional service not from one rare person, but from every person they come into contact with, the results are incredible."

"It sounds too good to be true, "Aaron said. "No one ever leaves here unhappy?"

Ross smiled. "Sure, sometimes people leave here unhappy. That's usually because some people are only able to be unhappy. Heck, I'm sure we all know people who are happiest when they are miserable. What we do at 'Customer's Paradise' is care about even the people who are not able to be happy. We care about every one of our customers...and we also care about each other. Everyone I meet is my customer, which includes co-workers and employees. As long as we all remember that fact then it consistently results in a great place to work and a spectacular place to eat."

"I understand. Thank you so much for taking the time to teach me this lesson, Ross."

"It was my great pleasure to meet and talk with you, Aaron. Are you hungry? Let me buy you lunch."

Aaron got up and moved with Ross towards the office door. "That sounds great. Thanks!"

"Well." said Ross looking slyly at Aaron as he held the door open for him. "Lunch is the least I can do for you. You're a platinum and I think we both know that you saved my restaurant today."

"Really?" Aaron asked with an innocent expression on his face. "How did I do that?"

"Well, when we met earlier, I told you I would close down the restaurant if we had met before and I didn't remember. I knew that we had met before, and I'd bet money that you also remember meeting me, yet you pretended that we had never seen each other.

Why did you go along with my story when you knew it wasn't true?"

Aaron grinned. "I left that fact out because you would have closed down the restaurant. Even though we had just met, I guess you could say that I cared about you...you and everyone else who comes to eat and work here."

Ross nodded and gently slapped him on the back. "Let's grab some lunch."

# Chapter 3

Aaron pulled up to the address listed on his current gold apple card, Al's Corner Gas. He had to stop on the road to wait for cars in front of him to pull into the actual gas station area; it looked like an extremely busy place. While he was waiting for an attendant to direct him to a free lane as it became available (a man waving a red flashlight as if on an airport runway), Aaron made a few observations. The first thing he noticed was that instead of being located on a corner, Al's Corner Gas was situated in the middle of the block. There was an entrance and an exit, both clearly marked, so that traffic would all enter from the same direction and exit in a similar fashion. There were eighteen gas pumps, arranged in three rows of six. Aaron noticed that this was a full service gas station, a rare occurrence in today's age of "do-it-yourself". He expected that gas here, at a full-service station, would be priced higher. That's how it was in the past when full service stations were more plentiful. Most would say that the higher price was one of the reasons that gradually, the full-service stations had been replaced by more economical self-serve gas bars. But Al's Corner Gas was charging the same prices for gas as a self service station. Aaron pulled into a vacant parking spot and walked into the store area, which was smaller than most by today's standards.

A very friendly cashier greeted him as he walked in. "Hi how ya doing today, Sir?" asked the cheerful girl.

"I'm doing well thanks. My name is Aaron and I'm here to meet with Jenn. She's expecting me." Jennifer was the owner of Al's. Aaron had called earlier and set up an appointment to visit.

"Oh yes Aaron!" the girl said excitedly. "We've been expecting you. Jenn wanted me to make sure that you had gotten gas from us before you meet. Have you ever been our customer?"

Aaron frowned. "No, I haven't. I'll go get in line and then come back in here when I'm finished?"

The girl nodded. "That would be perfect. My name is Nancy. When you come back in, ask for me or Jenn and we'll be sure to get you right into your meeting with her. I hope you enjoy the experience!"

Aaron thanked her and walked out the front door, chuckling at Nancy's enthusiasm. As he walked back to his car and got into line to wait for an open gas pump, he wondered what could be so exciting about getting gas.

After a very short wait, a pump became available. Aaron pulled up to the gas pump, rolled down his window, and turned off his vehicle. The ignition was barely off as the flurry of activity began. A young man wearing a headset walked up to the Aaron's window.

"Hi there, welcome to Al's! I'm Dave." Then he paused as if to ask, "and you?"

"Aaron."

Dave smiled. "Good to meet you Aaron. Fill 'er up?"

Aaron nodded. "Yes please."

Dave made a signal and Aaron noticed in his side view mirror that another teenager had already begun to pump gas. "Ok, Aaron, Mike has started to fill your car with regular gas now. If you want to pop the hood, Chris will check your fluids and oil. Your pit stop with us today will take about another six minutes. Can we bring you anything from inside our store? We have assorted chocolate bars available for the price of two for $2, and bottled water three for the price of two at $2."

Aaron thought about it for a second. "I could use an orange juice and a protein bar."

Dave paused for a minute as if listening to someone. He had a small microphone and earpiece on. "Both are on the way out, Aaron. Can Tim go ahead and give your interior a quick vacuum? It looks clean already, but it never hurts to get rid of the road dust?"

"Sure, why not." said Aaron. Another young man smiled at Aaron in greeting as he opened the passenger door and immediately went to work with a small but powerful sounding hand vacuum. He was very quick, efficient and respectful of the car's interior.

"Ok, Aaron, I think we're about done with the gas, under the hood, and with the vacuuming." Dave held out his hand and produced a small bottle of orange juice and a high quality protein bar. "Chris is telling me that your oil and all other under the hood fluids are at acceptable levels. Your wind shield washer fluid was down around halfway, but we always fill the washer fluid on the house. The gas tank is full and the dust is gone." Dave looked at his watch and adjusted one of the buttons. "Total time in our pit today is 6 minutes 22 seconds. Here is your bill." He then produced a bill which had printed out from a handheld point of sale machine hanging from his hip. The bill was itemized and had a total of $42.76 for the gas, orange juice, and protein bar. "Do you want to put that on your Al's card or pay by some other method?"

"I'll put it on my other card today, Dave." He fished his credit card out of his wallet and handed it to Dave. Dave accepted the credit card and handed Aaron a pamphlet in return.

"Ok Aaron, give me about thirty seconds to run this through and we can get you on your way."

Aaron checked his mirrors. Mike, Chris, and Tim had moved back to the next car and were repeating their activities with that customer. In front of that car was a different "Pit Boss" as he had come to think of Dave. Looking in his rear view mirror, he spotted Dave standing at the window near the cashier, likely waiting for the card to be processed. There were two other people that also had headsets on and were casually talking to Dave, waiting to process payments for customers of their own. Aaron looked at the pamphlet he had been handed. It was an application form for an Al's Gas card. A small gold apple was located in the bottom right portion of the application.

Dave came back and handed a receipt to Aaron. He also gave Aaron a car sized garbage bag that had a message printed in blue letters saying, "Thanks for stopping at Al's! We hope you come back when either you or your car get thirsty again!"

"Here you go Aaron." Dave said with a friendly smile on his face. "I hope to see you again next time you need gas and you're in the area." Aaron inspected the credit card slip and saw that there was no section for a tip. He quickly reached into his pocket and handed Dave a five dollar bill. "Thank you Dave. That was great service! I'll be back for sure."

Dave grinned. "Thanks Aaron, my crew and I really appreciate the tip. I just heard from Nancy that you're going in to meet with Jenn now. When the car ahead of you exits to the left please turn to the right and you'll find additional parking spots. I hope you have a great day."

Aaron nodded and thanked Dave again for his great service. He then did as instructed and when the car ahead of him exited he pulled his car into an available parking spot.

Aaron walked towards the front door of the store at the same time as another customer. Aaron got to the entrance slightly ahead of the woman and held the door open, stepping to the side so that she could enter before he did. He couldn't help but notice a dark wet stain on her coat and a distressed look on her face.

"Oh no," Aaron said. "A bit of coffee spilled in the car?"

The woman nodded. "Yes. I hope I can rinse it out before it sets in."

"Well if it's stubborn, I can recommend a great dry cleaner that performs miracles on stains." Aaron reached into his pocket and withdrew a business card. "Here you go. I was there a day or two ago and I always pick up an extra card in case someone is in need. Tell them Aaron sent you and said they were magical. They should get a kick out of that."

The woman smiled and accepted the card. "Thank you very much. If it doesn't come out I'll take it there. Have a good day." She then walked towards the restroom, waving to Nancy as she passed by. Nancy waved back and said something that Aaron couldn't make out. The lady laughed and entered the restroom.

Aaron approached the counter, noticing a man and woman standing near the register talking to Nancy. They both smiled and stopped talking when Aaron approached. The woman stepped forward, extending her hand towards Aaron.

"Well, I see you put the first Gold Apple rule of customer service into practice with no effort at all. You're treating my customers with coffee stains as if they were your customers. Well done! Hi Aaron, I'm Jenn."

Aaron shook hands with Jenn, who appeared to be in her early thirties. She was a fit woman; about five foot six, wearing a casual outfit of khaki pants with a Blue Al's Corner Gas golf shirt. "Hey Jenn. Good to meet you. Yeah I guess that was Rule #1 in action. But I've been treating people that way for as long as I can remember. I figure, if you can help a person have a better day, you should.

"I couldn't agree with you more. Are you all gassed up and ready to go?"

"Yes, I sure am. I have to admit that when Nancy sent me out to get gas, I was a bit confused as to what could be so special about the experience. But all I can say is, Wow! That was much different than a regular trip to the gas station. I wish you had this place closer to where I live. I would gas up here exclusively. Do you have a pretty large and loyal clientele?"

Jenn nodded, a bright smile on her face. "Yeah, we're proud to have a lot of regular customers here at Al's. Why don't you come on back to my office and we can chat a little about that gold apple card of yours."

They walked through the small store towards Jenn's office, stopping briefly en route to get a coffee. As they entered the office, Aaron noticed immediately that the desk configuration was the same as Ross's had been at the restaurant: the desk against the wall and both chairs side by side. Jenn closed the door, invited Aaron to take either seat, and then dropped down comfortably into the remaining chair. Taking a slow sip of her coffee she looked interestedly at Aaron.

"So, no offense Aaron, but you look older than 17. That means you're likely too old to be here for a job. Of course I could be wrong, so let me ask formally. You have a gold apple card, so a job here is yours if you would like one. We'd be glad to have you join the team. What do you say, wanna be a pit boss?"

Aaron shook his head with a smile. "Thanks for the offer, but no, I don't think I'm here for a job. This place looks like it's a lot of fun to work at, and I'm sure I could learn a lot. I would love a franchise of this gas station though. Is that a possibility?"

Jenn nodded. "It could be. Al's Corner Gas is not a big chain of stores. We like to keep it small because it's really very difficult to grow big as a company and keep a small company mindset which, we believe, is one of the keys to Al's success. This location is the second Al's and we haven't been around very long—only a year actually. So let me ask you a couple of questions to determine if you're here to be offered a franchise. First of all, are you a platinum apple card recipient?"

Aaron nodded.

"Great!" Jenn exclaimed. "Did Al give you the platinum card and send you here?"

Aaron shook his head. "No, I've never met Al. Actually I was guessing that was just an imaginary name once I heard your name was Jenn. I figured it was a private joke, just like this place is called a 'corner gas' but isn't located on a corner."

Jenn laughed out loud. "Yes the corner gas name is an intentional joke, but Al is a real person. Al is the founder of the original Al's Corner Gas, which is also not located on a corner. When Al opened the first location he figured that most full service gas stations didn't really give much in the way of service. He said, "If they don't mind falsely calling themselves full service stations, which is very important, then why would they worry about smaller details, like properly naming the location of the actual station?" So Al purposely called it a corner gas station, and made sure to get the full service part of the business accurate. It's a little joke that our customers get a kick out of. Anyway, if Al didn't send you, then my best guess is that you're not here to get a new location. I could be wrong about that though, so if you're truly interested, I can contact Al and find out for certain. Who did give you the platinum card and send you?"

Aaron briefly told Jenn about meeting Steve and getting the platinum card. Jenn nodded and listened while Aaron outlined his journey up to this point. "And that's how I find myself sitting in front of you now. Does that help at all Jenn?"

"It sure does. " Jenn replied. "If anyone asks you in the future, just say you're a platinum card from Steve. That'll let everyone know what to do with you." She smiled and paused. "That sounds a bit ominous doesn't it?"

Aaron laughed. "It does sound clandestine and mysterious. But I'm getting used to that."

"Well, don't worry. Nothing bad can come from this for you...only good things. Now I know why you're here. You're here to learn about the second rule of service. So, when you went to visit Ross he taught you about the first rule? That's where I went to learn it, too. I'd be surprised if there was a better place that exemplified the first rule."

"**Answering the primary question;** Do You Care About Me?" Aaron said. "Yes it's where I went to learn that, and you're right. Everyone there really does answer that unspoken question correctly. Never in my life have I been to a place where every single employee gives such great and complete customer service. It was a treat to witness."

"Perfect! You can expect to find the same level of service at any establishment where you see a gold apple displayed. On the flip side of things, if you go to a place and get this kind of excellent service but you can't find the gold apple symbol displayed, then please contact Steve immediately to let him know you've found a new candidate. There are some rare businesses, and many individuals, out there who are gold apples. Most of them still haven't been discovered. We all love to find them and bring them into the spotlight."

Aaron paused in thought, and then looked at Jenn seriously. "I've never heard about the Gold Apples until a couple weeks ago when Steve handed me the platinum card. Yet you're talking about it like it's some large organization. What can you tell me about it? Is it a corporation? Is Steve the founder? Or owner? What exactly are these Gold Apple businesses?"

Jenn took a sip of her coffee and then leaned forward in her chair. "Ok, Aaron, since you asked I will try to answer your question. This isn't really my specialty... "The Gold Apples Talk" as I like to call it. Steve is the master and he'll cover it much better when you finally meet up with him. But I'm sensing that you want information in order to go further, am I right?"

"Yeah," Aaron said. "I'm getting a feeling like this is some sort of secret society or something. I'm not really creeped out, but I'd like someone to give me some reassurance...otherwise I think I'll probably start feeling more uncomfortable."

Jenn laughed. "Well in a way it is a secret society..... but not on purpose."

"I'm confused," Aaron admitted.

"Okay, let me explain. Actually it's more like a movement, one that has only recently been organized and is rapidly growing because good things tend to create even more good things. I don't think it would be a terrible thing if there were more excellent restaurants or hotels or even gas stations in the world, do you?"

"No, I can't think how that could be bad." replied Aaron.

"I agree with you," Jenn continued. "Over the past five or six years, Steve and a few others like him have been going around finding, teaching, and encouraging excellent customer service. They find a "gold" apple and they give him or her a gold apple card. Then that gold apple is encouraged to go where she/he can gather with other likeminded people. Gold Apple establishments are beginning to pop up in all areas of industry and commerce. They all share a common trait which is phenomenal success in their marketplace. How does that sound to you?"

"Yes, I think I understand what you're getting at," Aaron replied. "It sounds very intriguing. Gold Apples are being picked and then placed together and the result is that the businesses they are populating are going on to be successful. So far I've seen a restaurant that's the best in the city, as well as a gas station that's like nothing I've ever experienced before. I wasn't there long, but I would like to hazard a guess that my first stop, the jewelry store, is also a Gold Apple establishment?"

"Bob's place? Oh yes, that's one of the shiniest gold apple establishments of the whole bunch! Ask around and you'll be amazed to hear how far people travel to buy jewelry from there."

"That's it in a very basic nutshell." Jenn stated. "Like I said, Steve covers the history much better than I can, and I should save that for him to tell you about."

"Alright," Aaron sat forward, feeling better for getting some explanation about the Gold Apples. "I think I'm ready to hear the second rule of customer service."

Jenn also sat forward. "Here it is. "The second rule of customer service is answering the unspoken question; Is it easy to do business with me?" Simple but powerful, just like the first rule."

Aaron nodded his head in agreement. "Sometimes it's the simple things that are most important. I can totally see how Al's Corner Gas is the place to come and see this rule in action."

"Do you really think so?" asked Jenn. "What were you able to observe during your experience with us that demonstrated the second rule of customer service?"

Aaron laughed. "Well, I imagine you already know the answers...but here goes. First, from the time I entered the gas area until the time I came back to your office, each and every person I came into contact with showed me that it was easy to do business with them. Pumping one's own gas is normally required in today's world. Al's Corner Gas helped me park and find a gas pump, and then the staff pumped my gas for me, and offered to bring me snacks as well! Then you cleaned my car interior and checked all the fluids under my hood. I never make time for that when I do the fill-up myself. You did all of these things...and you did them in less time than it would have taken for me to simply pump a tank of gas! I was impressed that you were a full-service gas station to begin with, but you went far beyond that and offered me much more than I would normally require. You also tied the first rule of customer service into my experience."

Jenn smiled slyly. "I don't think we did. Did we?"

"Of course you did," Aaron continued. "You showed me that you care about me by doing little things for free that normally cost money at other stations. If I want to vacuum my car at another place, I have to do it. I also have to pay to get the vacuum to turn on. Then there's the topping up of windshield washer fluid. Normally I must purchase a full container and pour it myself. Your guys took care of both these issues quickly and with no cost to me. Someone here realizes that providing seemingly small services can produce very grand results in the form of overwhelming customer satisfaction."

"You're right." Jenn agreed. "One of Al's famous quotes is, 'The day I need fifty cents so badly that I have to charge a customer for a quick vacuum, is the day I close the doors.' Most people say that if you take care of the pennies, the dollars take care of themselves.

Al believes that if you try to save a penny at the expense of the customer, it will cost you many dollars. He has developed ways to provide the very best for his customers while still making enough profit to be able to stay open. His success seems to prove that he's on the right track. Not many gas station owners make more than a million dollars a year from their business...but Al does." Jenn leaned forward in her chair. "Please keep that bit of information confidential. You get to hear that only because you're Platinum."

Aaron let out a low whistle. "You're right Jenn, that's pretty impressive. And I'll keep it to myself. Thanks for trusting me with confidential information."

"So the Second Rule of Customer Service is an unspoken question that must be answered each and every time I interact with customers. Is it easy to do business with me? Do I understand this correctly?"

"Yes that's it."

"Great. Do you mind if I ask you a few more questions, Jenn? I'm afraid at times I'm not too bright and I ask questions to make sure I understand things clearly."

"I'd be surprised if that's true, Aaron. You appear plenty bright to me. Of course, go ahead and feel free to ask me questions. I'm happy to answer them."

"What I saw today seemed pretty busy. Is this a busier than usual day or normal?"

"It's this busy every day. Don't get me wrong, there are many periods that are slow as with any gas station, we just don't have as many of those times. And in general, our slow times are busier than our competitors' busy times. Al's true strength, however, is that during peak busy times we're able to move a very high volume of cars through our pumps. We also have a very loyal customer base which rewards us with significantly more repeat and referral business than an average gas station. People really appreciate what we do for them, and when it comes time to get gas, many of them drive the extra distance to get to us."

"How much money do you spend paying for the "free perks" that you give to your customers? The washer fluid and vacuuming and any other things you might do?" Aaron asked.

"That's a good question, Aaron. But I'm not sure what the current price tag is on that."

Aaron was puzzled. "Is that good business practice? What if you're spending more money on these things than you realize and it's causing you to be less profitable at the end of the day?"

"The little extras that we provide might seem like a big expense, but they really aren't." Jenn shrugged good-naturedly. "Let me assure you, we're not losing money. I know how much everything costs; I just don't focus on it. I focus on how we can enhance a customer's experience at Al's while making sure we can be profitable. If we couldn't do these things and make money, then we'd be out of business. You're welcome to come spend a week with me and I'll explain everything you've experienced here. I'd love the chance to show off more, but that isn't why you came to me today."

"I don't focus on how much we're spending for washer fluid and vacuum cleaners because it's a small price to pay to make it easy to do business with us. I believe eliminating these services would truly be the costly approach. Have you ever been to a restaurant that has cloth napkins for years, and suddenly on your next visit you notice that they've switched to paper napkins? A little thing, really, and the customers don't immediately stop coming to eat there because of the change. Still it's a small, subtle message isn't it? "Dear Customer, we're saving money at your expense." Now I realize that many people would say it's not a big deal to get paper napkins instead of cloth. Ask people which they would rather have though, the answer is most often the cloth."

Jenn finished her coffee with a backwards tip of her head. "It's really all about 'show vs. tell' when it comes to customer service though. I choose to believe that the extras make more customers stay loyal to Al's."

"I think the same way you do." said Aaron. "What was that you just said? Show vs. tell? Do you mean show and tell like we used to do in grade school, or were you about to share another rule of customer service with me?"

Jenn's eyes lit up, and she sat forward on the edge of her chair. "No one has mentioned 'show vs. tell' to you." It was a statement not a question. "Great! I'll tell you all about it. But before I start, my coffee needs a refill, how about yours?"

They walked back to the front counter and poured more coffee. In all the time Aaron and Jenn had been talking in her office, the volume had stayed very busy at the gas pumps. Aaron commented on the traffic to Nancy, who was processing a credit card for one of the pit bosses.

"This isn't busy, just steady," Nancy replied.

Jenn offered Aaron a snack, which he selected from a tray of items that appeared to be free for the staff, and they both walked back towards the office.

"Free snacks for the employees?"

"That's right." said Jenn. "Free snacks, pop and coffee. And pizza is on me if you work a six hour shift."

"That seems very generous."

Jenn laughed. "I guess so. But it's also good for business. It's amazing how many of our kids actually want to work a six hour shift here, when most places find it hard to get their staff to even show up to work. "This is a fun place to work." Jenn continued. "We all work hard and enjoy doing it. I care about the staff, and I also want to make it easy for them to do business with me. Everyone here is my customer and as long as we're prosperous and doing well, it makes sense that they get some good benefits. The pay is better than any comparable gas station's, but even that's not a big paycheck. So we try to include some other perks that can help make the hectic pace more worthwhile."

Aaron was impressed. "I guess you also have no staff getting upset and stealing the odd bag of chips or pop this way either. I would imagine that happens in most stores?"

Jenn nodded. "Oh sure, I think that happens in other companies, but definitely not here. That's an accidental benefit for the company, but by no means was it the reason we decided to offer the free stuff. When the bottom line is viewed however, you're right. We likely spend less by giving our staff more treats than the stores that pay little and give nothing. Our team loves the benefits, and listing us on a resumé is great for their future as well. But the main reason they come work here is for the chance to land a bigger job."

Aaron's curiosity was piqued. "Do you mean a chance to land a bigger job within this company?"

"Well, it's true that people do advance here quickly. Everyone starts off by pumping gas. Then they move from that to checking under the hood, to vacuuming, and then to pit boss. Every shift has a crew chief who's also a pit boss, but also responsible for handling any unique concerns that might arise. The bigger jobs that I'm referring to, though, are job offers from our customers."

"Really?" Aaron asked. "What kinds of job offers come from your customers?"

Jenn smiled proudly. "Oh there are so many I wouldn't know where to start. Some of our colleagues from other Gold Apple companies come by regularly. If they find someone they want, then an offer is made. Usually we say goodbye to a great employee and off they go to make more money and help even more people. But it's not just Gold Apple establishments that come to recruit. If you watch the traffic moving through here for any length of time you'll notice a large volume of very expensive cars coming in. Often there are presidents and other influential people sitting in those cars. A lot of our employees are so good at providing customer service that they are offered much better jobs that are impossible to pass up."

"I'll share the story of a recent graduate of ours named Ken, for example. Over the space of a year and a half, Ken moved up the ranks until he was a crew chief. Then about three weeks ago, he was offered a job from one of our customers. Today Ken is a manager at a Fortune 500 company. His role is to hire and train a new customer service force to help turn around a troubled department. He's currently making a six figure income, and I would guess that over the next few months he'll be recruiting others from here to help him. Not too bad for a 20 year old guy, if you ask me."

"Are you serious?" Aaron couldn't believe what he was hearing. "A young guy working at a gas station is offered a job making that kind of money?"

"Absolutely." replied Jenn. "He was personally hired by the president of the company, a great guy who has been a customer of Al's Gas for quite some time. He was just in to get gas yesterday and, from what I'm hearing, Ken is surpassing all the expectations set for him so far."

"If other businesses keep hiring your staff, how do you keep the quality of service so high and also retain enough staff to work for you?"

"It's tough the first few months while you build your initial customer and employee base, but once you get the whole team in place it becomes easier. On average, about one or two people leave us for better opportunities every other month or two. That's not really so bad from a staffing perspective, since hiring new staff isn't difficult for us. Many of the people who work here have friends who can't wait for the opportunity to be employees here too. It's true that similar types of people group together. There are a lot of great young people out there and they associate with similarly great people. The senior staffers lead and train the newcomers. The original Al's really did an outstanding job of coming up with a successful training/mentoring system, and we use it at this location as well. Also, because we know that we have a high positive turnover, we're always accepting resumés and interviewing people. Often there's a waiting list to work here. There is right now."

"That's incredible."

"I can't believe it myself sometimes. Another benefit of constantly hiring good people is that fresh new ideas are always coming in. We are always coming up with original and creative ways to provide excellent service."

Aaron sipped his coffee. "Well I have to say, Jenn, this seems like a really cool business to be involved in. I think I took you off-topic though. Our coffees are almost gone and I remember hearing something about show and tell class."

"Yes, that's right! Show vs. tell."

"Show vs. Tell," Jenn began, "is not officially a Gold Apple rule of customer service. It's more like a Gold Apple philosophy. Show vs. tell can be seen in every interaction between people and it's a very powerful force in relationships. Being aware of it can help in so many ways."

Jenn walked over to a white board and wrote "Show vs. Tell" at the top. Then she wrote down some popular phrases. She resumed her conversation by reading the phrases out loud.

"Talk is cheap. Actions speak louder than words. Everyone has heard these sayings, or something similar. Show vs. Tell is just another way of expressing the same idea. Really the message of show vs. tell is this; **what people "do" is more accurate than what people 'say.'"**

"You said 'show & tell' earlier." Jenn said. "Let's use that as an analogy for what I mean. My daughter takes a toy fire truck in for show and tell at school. When it's her turn to present, she walks up to the front of the class and displays the toy fire truck for everyone to see. Then she spends the next five minutes telling everyone about the great item that she has brought in: a doll. She can talk as long and as much as she wants about her fun doll, but the reality is that she's showing everyone a toy truck. Now matter what she tells the class, what she shows them is far more important. After she sits down if you ask anyone in the class what she brought in for show and tell, the response will be unanimous: she brought in a toy fire truck."

Aaron smiled. "I see what you mean."

"Now let me give you a practical example that would relate to customer service and day to day business." Jenn offered. "Let's look at a regular company and their telephone customer service department. This company claims that help from them is only one short phone call away. Do you have a problem? Then they can help fix it. Simply call their hotline! Live, friendly operators are standing by to get you to a quick and easy solution. Assistance is available to you 24 hours a day, 7 days a week. This is what they tell you."

"You've recently purchased one of their products and discover that you need help, so you decide to call their heavily promoted helpline. Remember that they promised you live, speedy help. Here's how your call goes.

1. Your call is immediately answered...by an automated operator who gives you ten choices to direct you to the appropriate person to help you.

2. After going through the list (twice actually) you don't find the exact department you need, so you pick the one that sounds as close as possible.

3. You're transferred to another queue and placed on hold. A recording begins a loop and every thirty seconds it asks you to remain on hold. It also tells you how much your business (and call) is appreciated. There are times throughout your wait that you consider hanging up and trying again a bit later. Usually, just as you're about to hang up, a message tells you "Please don't hang up. Your call is important and we don't want you to lose your place in the current queue." The fear of having to go through this whole process again keeps you from hanging up and you continue to hold.

4. 14 long minutes later, just when you're ready to abandon all hope, a live voice comes over the phone! Sure the voice sounds bored and unhappy, but at least it's a real person! Finally you're close to getting your issue resolved!

5. The person on the other end of the line mumbles his or her scripted and insincere greeting, and then waits for

you to say what you need. It takes you a couple of seconds to remember what you're actually calling about, because it's been so long since you first called, but quickly enough you manage to convey your question to the help line employee.

6. In a voice that says, "wow, you're really wasting my time here", he tells you that he doesn't help with that particular problem. You should have pressed 8 instead of 10. It seems that the employee feels they have done all they can for you, because before you can ask them to connect you directly to the other department, they disconnect you. Or worse, if you do actually get to ask them to transfer you, they haughtily inform you that their phone system doesn't let them do transfers. Then they disconnect you.

"You sit there and look at your phone. Half an hour has passed since you began this call and you're still no closer to getting help. Do you have the energy to call again? Do you have another half hour to sit on hold, just to risk being told that you've selected the wrong option once more? 'Maybe my problem isn't so bad,' you tell yourself. "I guess I can live with it until I have time to call again or it gets worse.' This scenario can end in a multitude of ways. The important fact is that it ends poorly for you, the customer, and almost every time." Jenn paused, turning expectantly to Aaron.

"It's too bad that your example actually happens," Aaron replied. "I bet that I could ask anyone I meet about calling a help line, and they'd tell the same story, exactly the way you just did."

Jenn nodded. "You're right. Most companies 'tell' you that they want to help you quickly and easily. Yet when it comes time to deliver on their commitments, they 'show' you that they're not interested in helping you at all. I could come up with hundreds of examples of people 'telling' each other one thing, while 'showing' the exact opposite. To add insult to injury, the company you called really believes they provide great help and service. They have no idea how bad they are at customer service and won't do anything to improve it."

"Show vs. Tell." Aaron nodded. "I like it. Catchy phrase and it quickly conveys the philosophy. So you're saying that the action really is more important than the words."

"Of course." said Jenn. "This has been true for as long as people have communicated aloud. Show vs. Tell is nothing new, but it's very, very important to be aware of, for those of us that want to provide excellent customer service. Most people aren't conscious that, almost every day, they say one thing and yet do something entirely different."

Jenn looked at the clock on the wall. "I've kept you too long I think. I hope I've given you some good information, Aaron."

Aaron stood up and shook hands with Jenn. "The time flew by for me, Jenn. I appreciate you sharing these points. I could stay longer just to discuss Show vs. Tell."

"And I could sit here and talk about it for longer." said Jenn. "But I won't because this is something that will come up again and again so I'll let you get on your way. Any time you want to stop by for a chat, or want to call me and discuss anything, give me a call."

"What's the next step?" Aaron asked. "Or is there a next step?"

"Yes, there is definitely a next step." Jenn reached into her desk and pulled out three identical boxes. She thought for a moment, then opened one and removed a gold apple card, handing it to Aaron. Aaron examined it and observed that it was identical to the other gold apple cards he'd received, the only difference was a new address on the back of the card.

"The choice remains the same as always for you, Aaron. You can go home and continue your life, or you can visit the next address on this card and continue your Gold Apple experience. Off the record, from what I've heard and seen so far, I think you're one of the most platinum of all the gold apple card bearers that I've met."

Aaron smiled. "Thanks Jenn, I appreciate that."

Jenn opened the door to her office. As the two of them walked out she said, "I hope you continue your journey. When you're finished let me know what ends up happening in your life, I have a feeling that it's going to be something big."

"I will definitely continue." Aaron replied. "As for seeing me again, that's guaranteed. Now that I've had the royal treatment here at Al's I'm going to look for every opportunity to come back and get gas here!"

"Repeat business is the best compliment we can ask for." said Jenn, as she opened the door to the front parking lot for Aaron.

# Chapter 4

Aaron had discovered from the internet that the address on his new gold apple card belonged to a store by the name of Jake's Shoes. After his visit to Al's Gas Station, it seemed like a good idea to visit the location and experience the service before attempting to meet with his contact there. He needed a new pair of shoes anyway, he thought, so why not kill two birds with one stone?

Jake's Shoes was a big old house which had been converted into a store. The large parking lot behind the shoe store was full. As luck would have it, though, a car was pulling out to leave just as Aaron arrived. He parked his car, and then walked around to the front entrance. Before entering the store, Aaron stopped to look at the big sign for Jake's store in front of the house. In the bottom right hand corner of the sign there was the familiar Gold Apple logo.

Aaron entered the store and was once again pleasantly surprised to see that, similar to his experiences at the restaurant and gas station, this Gold Apple store was busy even though he had chosen what should normally be a slow time to drop in. Floor space throughout the store was separated into rows of shoe boxes piled high and stacked neatly. Cheerful employees walked around, offering to help customers. At a quick glance there looked to be about twenty customers shopping and five employees good-naturedly roaming around.

A man in his late thirties strolled towards the front door, a warm, ready smile on his face as he made eye contact with Aaron.

He calmly extended his hand. "Welcome back to Jake's Shoes! My name is Scott, and I have to apologize. I usually remember a face but, for the life of me, I can't recall your name."

Aaron shook hands with Scott, taking notice of the firm, confident grip. "No need to apologize Scott. We've never met before; this is my first visit to Jake's Shoes."

Scott leaned in towards Aaron, lowering his voice as he asked a question. "How do you feel about being the center of attention at times in your life?"

Aaron smiled with interest. "That type of thing doesn't really bother me. I've been in situations like that and never had a problem with it."

"Really?" Scott asked. "You're sure that twenty pairs of eyes suddenly won't be a problem?"

"Not at all." Aaron said reassuringly. "Why do you ask?"

Scott's smile broadened. He paused briefly, and then drew a deep breath. After about three seconds of inhaling, he bellowed out at the top of his lungs, "We have a first timer!"

Aaron jumped in surprise but, before he could do anything, the other five sales people on the floor and one behind the cash register all yelled out as one, "Welcome first timer! What is your name please?"

Aaron, smiling uncertainly, replied. "Thanks! My name is Aaron."

The sales people applauded and Aaron noticed that even the customers were clapping excitedly for him. Scott was also applauding as he called out for everyone to hear. "Welcome Aaron! To celebrate your first visit to our store everybody present gets half price off of every second pair of shoes for the next half hour! Who's glad to meet Aaron today?"

Everyone cheered one more time. Many of the customers were laughing and patting each other on the back. Aaron was embarrassed but smiled and waved. The cashier turned to a whiteboard behind her and wrote down in big letters, "Welcome Aaron!" She also wrote down the current time, and below it, another time exactly thirty minutes after the first one. Everyone was slowly going back to their business. A couple of customers that were close by said hi to Aaron and thanked him for coming in to buy shoes today.

Aaron couldn't believe it. Other customers were actually thanking him for coming to shop at Jake's! He could not help but marvel at the strategy behind this "First Timer celebration" event. The store was pleased because they had a new customer. The new customer was pleased because everyone had just cheered and applauded him/her. How could a person not feel special when something like this happened out of the blue? The other customers in the store also had cause to feel good because they were suddenly being offered a great deal on shoes! The owner of this store had taken a common promotion that almost all shoe stores implemented from time to time (buy one pair get the second half price) and made it into a fun celebration that got people excited. Jake's Shoes had certainly "showed" Aaron that they cared about him!

"So what kind of shoes are you looking for today Aaron?" Scott asked. He started to stroll slowly towards the men's shoe section. Aaron followed closely.

"I need a pair of cross trainers," Aaron said. "But before I try anything on, can I ask you a question or two about what just happened?"

"Of course." replied Scott. "Ask away. What size shoe do you take? You look to be about a 10?"

"Size 11," Aaron confirmed.

"What kind of cross training you going to be doing in your new size 11 cross trainers, Aaron?" Scott continued to ask questions in a very smooth, conversational tone.

"I jog around my neighborhood on the roads, and occasionally go to the gym to work out."

"Are you a heel striker or as light as air on your feet?" Scott inquired.

"I'm more like an elephant stampeding away from danger." Aaron replied.

Laughing out loud, Scott said, "I seriously doubt that, although you do paint quite the picture. Do you have any knee or joint problems that require special shoes?"

"Yes I have slight knee pain. I also fit into a wide shoe usually."

"Ok, that info is perfect. I have just the pair for you. Now let's see if I can remember where they are. You had a couple questions for me?" Scott prompted.

Aaron had almost forgotten that he did have a question, but quickly remembered what he had wanted to ask. "If I'd told you that I did have problems with being the center of attention, would this sale still be available?"

"Of course it would." Scott answered. "We would have just done the low key version. Nothing would have been said out loud, the word sale would be written on the board without your name, and each customer would be quietly told about the promotion on an individual basis. Some people just don't want to be centered out and we make sure to respect that."

"Do you do that every time a new customer comes in for the first time?"

Scott was peering at stacks of shoes for size 11 cross trainers. "Yeah, every first timer gets that treatment. Fun and deals for everyone! What did you think of it? Kind of entertaining, right?"

"Yes I really enjoyed the experience. As a matter of fact, I've never seen anything like it. Just because I come to shop here for the first time everyone present gets deals on their shopping. A couple of customers actually walked up to me as if the store belonged to them and genuinely thanked me for coming to buy shoes today. Most stores can't get employees to give that kind of sincere attention, yet here even the customers do it. That's utterly brilliant! "

"Good marketing too." Scott said.

"Without doubt." agreed Aaron. "You likely get people bringing in their friends and family just to get the 'first timer' prices. That must keep advertising expenses low." Scott nodded affirmatively. "I would also guess," Aaron continued, "that you don't have to do special sales all the time. If a customer wants a good deal on shoes they don't have to wait for a sale to be on when the store decides to offer one. It's up to them, the customer, to bring in someone new and the sale will instantly be available!"

"It sounds like you have a good eye for business, Aaron." Scott said as he opened a box of shoes and removed the packaging paper from inside the footwear. "The person that came up with the "first timer" promotion was pretty clever. Business is definitely booming at Jake's Shoes. The promotion never ends either, so customers can keep coming back over the years, which they continue to do. The service is pretty good here too. Actually, I'm being modest. The customer service here is great! Here, try these on and see what you think."

The shoes fit very nicely. They were comfortable, not too tight or restrictive. Scott told Aaron to walk up and down the aisle a few times to get a good feel for them. Aaron said he liked them so far but would like to try a few others on just to make sure.

"Absolutely we can try on some more, if you have the time for it, Aaron. I don't think you're going to find a pair that fit you better, but I don't mind being wrong. Let me get a few different brands for you to sample. Hey, do me a favor and walk around a bit with those shoes on. The longer you walk in them the more you can decide if they are good or not. If you come to a decision for buying a second pair of shoes for half price, then maybe you would like to pick a dress shoe or casual one? Feel free to stroll around and I'll give you a shout when I have a pile of cross trainers here for you."

"Good idea, Scott, thanks. I will walk around a bit and see if there is anything interesting. I think I'll likely just get the one pair, but hey, you never know."

While strolling around, Aaron happened to notice a pair of nice black dress shoes. He picked them up and thought about asking to try them on. They were sharp looking, and with the offered price discount, a great deal. Aaron made a mental note to try them on, but only on one condition; a sales person would have to ask him. So far the sales process was very low pressure. In fact, he felt no pressure to buy at all, but he wanted to see how the sales people at Jake's Shoes displayed their aggressiveness in selling. He expected that they would try to get him to buy more and he wanted to see how they could do that yet still make him feel comfortable. Aaron had often done this while shopping. Usually the result was that salespeople didn't even bother to ask him for more business. He was pretty sure that wouldn't be the case here though.

Scott called out a few minutes later and Aaron went back to trying on cross trainers. Scott excused himself a few times to go help other customers, but he always returned to make certain that Aaron was taken care of. About half an hour, and eight more pairs of shoes later, Aaron had decided on the pair that he liked best.

"Well I have to admit you were right on the money, Scott." Aaron said. "The first pair you gave me to try on is the most comfortable. Sorry to make you go running around to get all those other shoes."

Scott didn't appear to be bothered. With a smile on his face he said to Aaron, "Hey that's no problem at all. I understand wanting to find the best fitting shoe. You're going to be spending a lot of time in them and I'd be happy to go get another ten pairs if you like. If you come back and buy twenty pairs of shoes from me, and each of them is the first pair I picked out, I still won't mind if on the 21st pair you want to try others on just to make sure. It's all good with me."

"Does that happen a lot?" Aaron asked. "That the first pair you choose is the best fit for your customer?"

Scott laughed. "Yes, with most customers I can pick the shoe they like very quickly. Even on a person's first visit I can most often pick the shoe that they will love on my first try. I guess I have a knack for that kind of thing. Was there any other shoe that caught your eye today or is this pair good enough?"

Smoothly done, Aaron thought to himself. "Actually I did see a pair of nice dress shoes. Since I'm getting the second pair for half price today I think I'll try them on."

"Good idea. Let's go over to the bench and try them on."

As they got close to the seat near the dress shoes, Aaron started to walk towards the specific shoe he had in mind. Scott said, "I already have the correct shoe and size sitting on the bench. When I noticed you looking at them earlier, I took a chance that you might want to try that shoe...so I went ahead and got it ready for you."

Aaron thanked Scott and walked to the bench. Sure enough the correct shoe was sitting there ready to be sampled. "Nice touch." Aaron thought to himself. "This guy is making it easy to do business with him for sure."

Aaron tried the shoes on and they fit perfectly. He told Scott that he would take them as well. They walked up to the cashier and Scott went behind the counter to stand beside the cashier.

"Mandy, our first timer is ready to cash out." said Scott. "How many customers did Aaron help get deals today?"

Mandy smiled and looked at the white board behind her. There were numbers written underneath the times and message that she had put up when Aaron had been welcomed to the store. "It looks like 14 pairs of shoes found very nice homes at half their regular price." She said with a smile on her face. "You made a lot of people happy today, Aaron, which makes all of us happy. Thank you so much!"

Aaron knew it was a bit of a gimmick, but he couldn't help feeling pleased and important. "Well it was my pleasure Mandy. I'm glad I could be a part of it."

"Ok Mandy, let's ring Aaron up. This pair of shoes is full price and the second is half." Scott stood off to the side a bit and let Mandy handle the cash register.

"Nice cross trainers!" Mandy exclaimed. "Aaron, I'm going to ask you a question only because usually the answer I get is no. Have you ever worn really good running grade socks to train in? Not the regular tube socks, but specially made running socks?" She held up a pair of socks that were displayed beside the cash register.

"No, I've never worn a pair of socks like that before." responded Aaron. "I always thought that they were just another way to get my money and had no benefits to them. Do they actually make a difference?"

"They really do." Mandy nodded seriously. "Today you could buy some with the money you saved on your second pair of shoes. I use them now exclusively when I'm running and the sweating and occurrence of blisters is greatly reduced. If you don't get them today that's definitely no problem, but you must really try them out sometime. You'll be glad you did."

Aaron smiled. "Ok, you're right. Today is the best way to try a pair, for the least amount of money out of my pocket, I'll take them." He had to admit to himself that these sales people were good. He didn't feel like he was being pressured at all. They were recommending the socks so that he could get a better running experience in their opinion. Aaron also guessed that if he didn't like the socks they would give him his money back. He asked Mandy about that, and she responded with a quick, "Of course you can, that's our policy for everything we sell here."

Mandy and Scott made some small talk as Aaron paid by credit card. He signed his card slip and Mandy handed him his newly purchased shoes.

Scott shook hands with Aaron one more time. "Thanks again for your business, Aaron. I hope you will come back and see us again soon."

"Scott, I can guarantee you that I'll be back next time I need shoes. I had a great experience here and will definitely tell my friends about this place."

"That's great to hear." said Scott. "Have a good day."

"Well," Aaron thought to himself as he unlocked his car door and pulled out of the still busy parking lot, "I seem to be getting a good list of businesses to buy from, even if I never find Steve."

# Chapter 5

Three days later Aaron was walking back into Jake's Shoe store to meet with his Gold Apple contact. When he had called to arrange the meeting he was surprised to learn who he would be meeting with. He was looking forward to this visit.

Mandy was standing at the cash register and she smiled in recognition as Aaron came into the store.

"Well hello there, Stranger!" said Mandy. "Back so soon? I hope those socks didn't disappoint you, but if they did then we can return them with no problem."

"The socks were an amazing recommendation Mandy. I'm glad that you suggested I try them out. I honestly don't think I'll wear anything else now when I'm running. So in order to cut down on the smell potential, please do me a favour and make sure I get at least two more pair before I leave today. I'm actually here for another reason though. I called earlier to set an appointment to visit with the owner."

Mandy nodded. "Okay, I'll remind you about the socks before you leave. The boss is in back at the moment but he should be out any second." she paused, looking towards the back of the store. "Well speak of the devil, here he comes now."

Aaron turned around and watched as Scott walked to the front cash register, a big smile on his face. His hand shot out and he shook hands warmly with Aaron.

"Welcome back, Aaron! I had no idea the other day I was selling shoes to a Gold Apple!"

Aaron returned the firm handshake and replied, "Hi Scott and thanks. I had no idea the other day that I was buying shoes from the owner himself."

Scott chuckled. "Yeah, I guess we both get a bit of a surprise. Well, I know you've already experienced our service...I recommend that before I meet with any Gold Apple. But if I'd known you were coming I would have given you a better salesperson, so you could get the truly good service."

Mandy snorted derisively in the background. "Oh please stop being modest, Scott. We all know he got the best service available." She looked at Aaron. "He's always bashing himself. I'm not sure if it's for the attention, or if he actually believes he's not as good as we all know he is."

Scott shrugged. "A little of both I guess. I like to think I'm pretty good and accolades from one's peers are also nice to receive sometimes. I believe that if a person thinks they are so great it usually turns out they aren't. Learning and improving only occurs when a person believes that they can still improve, and I'm positive that I can always become better."

"I like that way of thinking." Aaron said. "I feel exactly the same way."

"Well then, Aaron, I can tell that we shall get along well. Come on, let's go back to my office where we can talk a bit."

Aaron smiled at Mandy and followed Scott back towards his office. A quick glance at the whiteboard showed that a "First Timer" was in the store and a sale was in progress. Walking towards the back of the store Aaron took note of the busy atmosphere.

Once again Aaron entered an office that was, by now, a familiar looking set-up. This time he commented on it to Scott. "The desk and chairs of every Gold Apple office I enter are the same. Is that to reflect the rules of customer service and also to demonstrate the "show vs. tell" principle?"

"You're absolutely correct," said Scott. "We sit on the same side as our guests to show we're on the same side— their side—of any situation. We show them we care about them and are not their adversary, but a partner. It's also easy to do business with us this way. When a person is relaxed then it's easier to have a conversation and get things done. So we're here for me to tell you about the Third Rule of Customer Service, right?

"That would likely make sense. I know the first two. Are there other things that you teach when a Gold Apple comes your way?"

"Other Gold Apples, yes." answered Scott. "For Platinum Gold Apples, however, it's definitely the Third Rule I cover."

"What makes you think I'm a platinum apple card holder?" asked Aaron.

Scott smiled confidently. "I'm in the loop. You came by the other day and I liked you. I thought you showed potential to get a gold apple card. When I called and told Steve that I had found a new candidate, he informed me that you'd already been given a card. He then went on to tell me that you were a Platinum and would be coming back to hear the third rule of customer service soon."

"What made you think I was worthy of a gold apple card?" asked Aaron. I didn't give you any customer service."

"Well, after a while, we just start to see certain qualities that identify you as a Gold Apple candidate." Scott stated. "In your case, you were a great customer. You made it easy to do business with you. You know what I mean?"

Aaron nodded in agreement. "Yeah, I can agree with that. I think that in order to give great customer service a person has to be a good customer themselves. I often have positive customer service experiences and can't help but feel that I was the one responsible for steering it that way. I think that I make it easy to sell to me because I understand what I need, and am also open to having a fun experience while I'm buying. Maybe that comes through."

"It really does. That was what I saw in you. You also asked good questions and by asking them you showed that you cared about me. You bought shoes from me but asked me about my business and also displayed interest in me. I had a great time selling to you!"

"Thanks Scott, I'm glad."

"So I was pleased to hear that you're a platinum card holder and are ready to hear about the third rule of customer service. Who have you talked to and what have they covered? I don't want to bore you with repetition if someone has already discussed a topic with you."

Aaron briefly told Scott about his visits with Bob, Ross, and Jenn so far. He explained that he had heard about the first rule of customer service, **Answer the question;** *Do* you care about me?, the second rule, **Answer the question;** Is it easy to do business with me? He also mentioned how Jenn had graciously added the bonus talk about the Gold Apple philosophy of Show vs. Tell.

Scott listened attentively and asked questions throughout Aaron's review, allowing Aaron to give an overview of his understanding of the information that he had been exposed to so far. Aaron concluded his story and Scott had a pleased look on his face.

"Well, Aaron it sounds like you've received some good sound information from my colleagues and have understood it all perfectly, which is excellent. If you stopped your journey now, you would have the basic building blocks for millions of dollars of success clearly tucked away in your head. Applying the first two rules of customer service and the philosophy of Show vs. Tell would enable you to do some very powerful things with a business. I would guess that you do these things naturally or you wouldn't be a platinum card holder." Aaron nodded in agreement. "However, now that you have this information in a concise form, you can share it with others—and in turn, they can take these success principles and also put them into action."

Scott paused for a moment and then asked a different type of question. "Are you having fun?"

The question took Aaron by surprise, but his reply was quick and confident. "Now that you mention it, yes I'm having fun. I've met some great people and, I hope this doesn't sound too conceited, but I don't feel alone anymore. It's refreshing to meet others who share my way of thinking."

"There have been times at past jobs where I was surrounded by people delivering exactly the opposite style of customer service from mine," Aaron continued. "In my opinion they weren't giving good customer service at all, but they would say that it was me doing things the wrong way, which made me feel like the crazy one. Even though my results were usually better than theirs, I would feel like I was speaking one language while everyone else was speaking another."

"I know exactly what you're talking about. When Steve found me, I was in that very same place. I've been a part of this organization for four years now. During that time I've met so many people that share our way of thinking. Plus I have a business that's fun to work at and is making more money than I ever dreamed possible."

Aaron laughed. "That sounds good to me! Do you have to work all the time or can you relax and spend some of that money?"

"I could work less I suppose. But it really is true that when you love what you do, it doesn't seem like work at all. I spend about three months of the year away from work though so it's not too grueling. But enough about me and my life, you came here to learn about one of my favorite topics! So if you're ready, I'll share with you the third rule of customer service."

"Sure." replied Aaron. "Do you mind if I take a guess at naming the third rule based on what I saw from you the other day?"

"Go for it." Scott said, smiling.

"Alright, thanks. The other day you were masterful at asking me questions to help select the right type of shoe for me. You were very natural and conversational in your style of asking questions, which makes me think that you do it often. I think the third rule of customer service deals with asking questions so that you can deliver the best customer service."

With an amused look on his face, Scott asked Aaron. "If I asked you to guess, if you had to give it a fancy catch phrase, what would the rule title happen to be?"

Aaron thought for a moment, and then announced his guess. "Well it would be something like; "Questions are Key". How did I do? Am I right?"

Scott pulled out a printed sheet and held it up for Aaron to see. His hand covered the first part of the message, but written at the top of the sheet on the right side was the following........ Questions are King.

"Aaron if this is the first time you've seen this rule then I'm glad Steve found you. You really are a natural at this stuff. That's quite the title for something so simple." Scott began. "It sounds like we're giving this rule the royal treatment."

Aaron smiled.

"And we are, for one simple reason," Scott continued. "Questions are the only way to eliminate what I consider to be the most destructive force in the world."

"That's pretty strong. Are we talking nuclear weapons or world hunger?"

"Something more destructive than those things," Scott replied. "In fact, the force I'm talking about is really the cause of such events."

"You have my full attention, Scott. What's this force?"

"The most destructive force in the world," Scott paused for dramatic effect, "is to make assumptions."

Aaron looked at Scott, puzzled. Scott continued to sit there and watch Aaron, waiting patiently for him to say something. As time passed in silence, Aaron began to think seriously about Scott's statement.

"You know, when you mentioned destructive forces, my first thought was nuclear missiles. But now that I think about it, I realize that a nuclear launch is most likely to happen as a pre-emptive strike...based on the assumption that the other side was about to launch first. So I think I understand what you're saying."

"Exactly." said Scott. "When people assume things and then act on those assumptions, terrible things can, and often do, happen. Think of one problem that occurs between people today and you'll find an assumption hidden in there somewhere. If you can accept this, which by the way, many people can't, then you will have gained a very powerful tool that can help you live a more successful life."

"Pick any example of a problem between two people and I can show you both an assumption, as well as questions to eliminate the assumption. Once the assumption has truly and completely been eliminated, agreement and understanding are all that can remain."

"If it were that easy, misunderstandings would become extinct," Aaron mused.

"Yes, they would." said Scott. "Sometimes it's not possible to eliminate all assumptions and get to understanding. Most often it is possible, yet in many cases people either don't ask enough questions, or they don't ask the right questions to eliminate assumptions. The average person is not a question asker, because they are either lazy or simply don't care. It's easier to obtain a couple of facts, impose their knowledge of past experiences to formulate conclusions, and then accept them as truth. This kind of process leads to incorrect assumptions and is just lazy, in my opinion, but it's what usually happens."

"I agree with that." Aaron nodded. "Many times I've seen people misunderstand what's happening and totally come up with the wrong conclusions."

"Can you give me an example?" asked Scott.

Aaron laughed. "Almost every interaction between people provides examples. Sure, let me think of one off the top of my head. Let me give you one from your very own shoe store."

Scott sat forward with interest. "Okay, that sounds great. Fire away."

"Alright here's a quick assumption. You have no back store room. This is an assumption based on the fact that your showroom is piled with shoe boxes. To add weight to my assumption, the other day when I came here, I didn't see any salespeople go into a back room to get shoes for customers to try on."

"Good so far, but how do you define assumption?" asked Scott.

"I call it an assumption because I've looked at the situation with my own eyes and come to a conclusion," Aaron began, "But I haven't asked anyone else if this is true or not, so it's really only an assumption."

"You're exactly right." said Scott. "That's a good example of an assumption, —and the assumption is wrong, by the way."

Aaron shrugged. "That's okay, I don't mind being wrong."

Scott paused at Aaron's statement and then nodded. "You don't mind being wrong because you're a Platinum. A person who's not afraid to be wrong, who's willing to admit that they don't know something is very, very rare and entirely relevant to this rule. Most people hate to be wrong. They're so afraid to be wrong that their subconscious won't even accept the possibility. It's that fear of being wrong that drives people to make assumptions. The average person convinces themselves that they are always right. So when they assume something, it takes almost no time for them to accept it as fact. How many relationships end badly simply because both sides involved refuse to accept the possibility that they could be wrong? The sad answer is: most of them."

"So the world is doomed then?" Aaron asked with concern in his voice. "If most people are afraid to be wrong and they allow themselves to make assumptions to avoid being wrong, then questions won't be asked and the world will be full of misunderstandings, pain, and sorrow...which it already is."

"Sure the world is doomed," Scott shrugged. "But it always has been. If you focus on the negative people and listen to their advice, then you will become negative like them. I'm a positive person so I focus on positive things. Negative people would tell you that a business like mine could never exist. They would say customer service isn't *that* important. These same people would also declare that the simple rules you've been shown are common sense and not worth taking the time to focus on. But for us the world is a positive place, businesses like mine do exist, and implementing the gold apple rules of customer service produce powerful results. It's these positive people that we want to find and help to grow. We call them Gold Apples."

"So now that I've talked about assumptions let me present to you the complete third rule of customer service." Scott said.

Scott held up the paper again and this time he didn't cover any of it. It read "Assumptions are bad....Questions are King!"

"So in a nutshell," Scott said, "assumptions are bad. Questions eliminate assumptions. Excellent customer service involves eliminating assumptions by asking questions, so that your customers are happy and both you and they know it. That's the third rule customer service of the Gold Apples?"

"How many questions do you need to ask?" queried Aaron. "There's not a set number or sequence of questions, is there?"

"I wish there were a set number, a magic formula, but of course there isn't." Scott said. "You need to ask questions until both people are crystal clear on what the customer means. Asking questions really is an art form. Most of the time they start out vague and, over time, both people will begin to ask more direct, straightforward questions. This happens as you get comfortable with the other person. It's not as simple as saying, "Ask eleven questions and you'll always remove assumptions. Also, you need to accept the truth that there is such a thing as a bad question. The other day you came in to buy shoes, so most of my questions were about shoes. If you'd told me you wanted to buy a running shoe, and I responded by asking you where you like to take your family vacations, that would have been a bad question."

"I see what you mean." Aaron said.

"Eventually," continued Scott, "We might talk about where you and your family take vacations. That would only happen once you'd come in a few times and felt comfortable enough to talk about that type of topic."

"What can a person do if they're not good at asking questions but they want to eliminate assumptions?"

"The same thing that a person can do for any aspect of their lives that they want to improve in," replied Scott. "They just have to practice, practice, and practice. Then realize they still have more to learn and practice even more. Practice asking questions until eventually you get good at it. People usually expect to try something once and succeed. They forget that to be really good at anything, a person has to practice continually and for a long time. It's a good thing we learn to walk when we're little. If we had to learn when we were twenty years old, all of us would give up after the first few tries and I'd have no shoe business."

They both laughed at the thought.

"I remember going to a self-help seminar years ago," Scott continued. "The speaker talked about the importance of asking questions. He stated that if a person could truly excel at asking great questions, then the world would be a happy, fulfilling place for that person and those around him. The presenter gave an example of a real life scenario, and then provided a whole series of questions off the top of his head that would help him understand the situation better."

"I remember sitting there watching that guy ask all of those questions with ease and thinking to myself, "There's no way I could ever come up with so many good questions." So I raised my hand and told him so. "The speaker smiled good-naturedly at me as if he had heard my excuse many times. Then he told me that anyone could get good at asking questions, if they wanted to, and practiced enough.

"So I took up his challenge," Scott continued, "mainly to prove him wrong. I envisioned going back to another seminar and telling him that I had followed his advice but still failed. His advice seemed so simple that I thought there was no way it could work.

"The only hitch with that dream," Scott laughed, "was that after about three months of intense practicing, I realized I was getting really good at asking questions. Not only was I good at it, but asking all these first-rate questions was significantly changing my life. I was so much better at my job and with people. I became truly interested in people and, because they sensed my sincere interest by the types of questions I asked, my personal and business success skyrocketed."

"Did you ever go back to thank the guy that gave you the advice in that seminar?" Aaron asked. "You wanted to blast him at first, but when it turned out he was right did you go back to tell him?"

"I sure did." Scott nodded. "I went up to him and told him my story. Then I thanked him for making such a positive change in my life. He told me that he didn't make the change; he'd simply shown me something that he had shown hundreds of others. He claimed I deserved all the credit for taking his advice and doing the most difficult thing, actually making use of it."

Scott paused, then pointed to a gold apple card which was framed and hanging on the wall near his desk. "I shook the speaker's hand and said, 'Thanks again Steve.' Steve told me that he was pleased to meet me and hear such a great success story, then he handed me this card."

"It was the same Steve that gave me my first gold apple card?" Aaron asked.

"Yes, Sir." Scott confirmed.

"So," Scott concluded, "Assumptions are bad. Questions are King. Any questions?"

Aaron laughed. "Yes quite a few actually."

"That's good. I'd love to hear them and so would someone else. If you can hang onto your questions for about 10 minutes it's time to take a quick drive to meet Steve." Scott smiled at the surprise on Aaron's face to hear this news. "Are you ready?"

Aaron nodded eagerly.

# Chapter 6

"Hi Rebecca, how are things today?"

The receptionist at Steve's office, smiled as Scott walked up to her desk and placed a coffee beside her phone. "Things are great, Scott. Am I ever glad to see you!"

"You felt like a coffee, right?" Scott said jokingly.

"Absolutely!" Rebecca nodded with a laugh. She looked from Scott to Aaron. "Hi there, you must be Aaron." she said. "I've been hearing some great stuff about you lately. It's a pleasure to meet you."

Rebecca shook hands with Aaron.

"It's very good to meet you too, Rebecca." Aaron said.

"You can go on into Steve's office, guys. He's expecting you."

Scott thanked Rebecca and then led Aaron past the reception desk towards a huge mahogany door that opened into Steve's office.

When they had driven up to this impressive building Aaron asked if Steve was a lawyer. Scott said that he wasn't, but that many lawyers would love to make even half the money that Steve pulled down in a year from his Gold Apple business. When Aaron had asked what type of business it was, Scott said he would let Steve reveal that.

The interior of Steve's office mirrored its exterior perfectly. The walls and floors were all adorned with dark marble, rich woods, and lush carpets. Steve was just standing up from a large black leather chair behind an expensive looking desk as the two men entered his office.

"Welcome gentlemen." Steve said, smiling warmly as he walked forward to shake hands with both of them. "Aaron, finally we meet

again! I trust you've found your journey through Gold Apple territory interesting so far?"

"Interesting would be an understatement, Steve." Aaron
replied. "Over the past couple of weeks I've met so many wonderful
people and seen businesses comprised entirely of individuals who
all enjoy their work. It's a refreshing change from normal businesses
where most employees are miserable, and the service is often
abysmal. I've found some great new places to shop at and, I must
admit, am disappointed that every place I need to buy from doesn't
have a Gold Apple logo on their sign. Learning the rules of customer service has been quite the education as well. Ross, Jenn, and
Scott were all excellent teachers. They made it not only easy to
learn, but fun as well!"

"That's great to hear, Aaron. I'm glad that you've had a good
time so far. Why don't we sit down and talk a bit. I imagine you
have questions. I can also tell you a bit more about the Gold Apples."

"I must admit that I'm a little confused." said Aaron. "This is
the first Gold Apple office where the desk isn't against a wall. If I
want to set up an office, which way would be best for me to place
my seating, so that my customer feels most at ease? The way I see it
here or at Jake's shoes?"

Steve laughed. "What a polite way to ask me if I disagree with
the other people's desk layouts."

Aaron smiled confidently. "I don't want to offend anyone and I
just learned that assumptions are bad and questions are king."

"Well done," said Steve. "To answer your question, the best way
to make customers at ease is to use the layout from the Gold Apple
offices. I get away with my desk placed the way it is for two reasons.
One reason is that in this size of office, I don't like to sit with my

back to the door. I always have a crazy feeling some bad guy is going to burst in and shoot me in the back. Yes, I know it's irrational, but the thought is there sometimes and it distracts me. Reason number two is that I only use that desk when I'm alone in here. For meetings, everyone sits together over there."

Steve pointed to a sitting area with a big screen TV and a bar. It looked like a small living room complete with end tables and two large dark brown leather couches that were angled together side by side, more like the arrangements in the other Gold Apple offices.

Aaron scanned the rest of the large office as he followed Steve and Scott over to the sitting area. There was another large space to the left, with a beautiful honey-coloured wood pool table and an additional big-screen television. In the total opposite corner he could see a professional-looking poker table surrounded by eight luxurious leather high backed chairs.

"This office is very handsome." stated Aaron. "It's much bigger than my apartment."

Steve boomed out a good natured laugh. He was 6 feet tall with an athletic appearance. Aaron guessed he weighed about two hundred pounds. Steve's dark short hair was graying just slightly at the sides. He was a solid man and the deep laughter came easily, as if he laughed often.

"You've got a point there. I think this office is about three thousand square feet, which makes it close to, or a bit bigger than, most average houses. I allow myself the space because I tend to spend a lot of time in here doing business as well as entertaining. I think it's a testament to the fact that exceptional customer service can pay well."

Scott and Aaron sat together on one couch and Steve sat on the other. They made small talk while opening the lids on their coffees and taking a few sips. Steve asked Aaron to give an account of his journey so far, requesting that he also include the rules of customer service as he had learned them from the business Gold Apples. After Aaron had recounted all that he had experienced, Steve nodded with a satisfied look on his face.

"Excellent work, Aaron," Steve said. "It sounds like our business Gold Apples did their usual impeccable job of sharing their information. Scott, Jenn, and Ross are three of the best teachers out there. I'll be sure to thank Jenn and Ross later today. Thank you, Scott for doing such a great job, as usual."

"It was my pleasure, as always." Scott replied. "I'm very interested to see what Aaron will be doing with us in the future. Do you have specific plans for him at the moment, Steve?"

"Not really," Steve shrugged. "But I know he's a sharp one and will soon be doing something interesting, I think even more exciting than anything I could choose for him to try."

"That's pretty confident." said Aaron. "I'm not sure if I'll be able to live up to such high hopes."

"Actually, I think the person in this room with the most confidence in Aaron," Steve was looking directly at Aaron, an amused expression on his face, "Is Aaron himself. It's good to be modest, but if you praise yourself in front of me I won't think you're being conceited."

The men sat and drank their coffee, making small talk and getting to know each. Eventually, Scott stood up to excuse himself.

"Well, boys," Scott announced. "My coffee is gone and I have to get back to the store. Lots of work to do today still for me, plus I have another Gold Apple appointment a half hour from now."

The men stood and shook hands one more time. Aaron thanked Scott for all of his help; Scott invited him to stop by the store any time. The two remaining men sat down as the door clicked shut.

"So Aaron," Steve began, "Now that you've shared your journey with me, would it be alright if I shared my story with you? I think you might find some of it interesting and, maybe it will answer a few of your remaining questions. Feel free to interrupt me if anything needs more clarification. I have no other appointments today, so I can give you as much time as you need."

Aaron nodded and Steve began to tell his story.

"My background is in sales and customer service. I discovered the benefits of self-improvement and lifelong education early in my career. They say that a person goes to college to learn a trade, and attends university to learn how to learn. I attended university for a couple years, and while I was there I learned one lesson that stuck with me: if you want to learn anything, you can't rely on others to teach you." He leaned back comfortably in his chair as he continued.

"Most of the teachers were there for the primary purpose of getting funding to do their own research. Teaching undergrad students was, to many of them, a bothersome price that they had to pay for getting that funding. If you wanted to get a good grade, you quickly realized that you were going to have to read your textbook and learn most of the information on your own. I decided to leave university before getting a degree, believing that there was more money for me working as a salesman. I almost certainly became more successful than most of my ex-classmates who did get a degree."

"As soon as I got my first job in sales, I went out and bought a couple books to learn as much as I could about the topic. One was written by Zig Ziglar, and the other by Dale Carnegie. I read both books fairly quickly and they both contained a lot of great material. They also challenged the reader to put their information into practice as quickly as possible. To start off with, I attempted some of the more ridiculous suggestions because I doubted that they could possibly work in the real world. My intention was to do the activities and prove they weren't achievable, but I soon found that the methods did indeed work! At first I was actually disappointed," Steve laughed. "But my disappointment soon turned to pleasure from the success that I began to experience."

"Today I passionately believe," Steve continued, "that a person should always seek to learn new things. My grandpa would say that a day where he didn't learn something new was a wasted day. I remember hearing another phrase early on in my life that's stayed with me as well: Success Leaves Clues. The people who have already succeeded at what we want to do can show us the way to prosper, if we are willing to look at their efforts and listen to their advice. Whenever I've wanted to learn something, the easiest and quickest route for me to take has been to gain knowledge from the experts. Books and tapes are a great way to do this because, through them, we can gain access to the wisdom of successful professionals we'd never have a chance to meet in our daily lives."

"So I spent a great deal of time learning from books and tapes. I found that this education and experience helped me to excel significantly over my peers in my chosen profession of sales."

"I also became quite good at public speaking and teaching," Steve said. "I get a thrill out of helping people, and as a salesman I was able to do that every day. Not many realize this, but the field of sales rewards those who are good at two things: self-directed learning and excellent customer service. If you are the cream that rises to the top of sales, it's most likely because you are skilled in these two areas."

"I'll skip telling you about the boring years that I read books and worked as a successful salesman," Steve smiled. "Maybe I'll write about them in a book of my own someday, if I ever get time."

"There often comes a time when a person is given the chance to be a manager. This opportunity is usually a result of being good at your job, and also being with a company long enough to have the seniority to be considered for the position. This happened for me about three years into one of my sales jobs. I accepted the position and then entered a new stage in my life."

"Being good at your original job doesn't guarantee that you'll be good in your new role as a manager. It's an entirely different creature, complete with its own set of challenges and skills to master. I look back on my record and have to conclude that I was a good sales manager. I was responsible for hiring and training a great team of young and inexperienced sales people. By the time I left that company, I had produced an aggressive, customer-service-oriented sales force that was responsible for six years of consecutive double-digit percentage sales growth. These were phenomenal sales numbers in a mature territory that upper management didn't expect at all. Every year they would question my sales growth forecast and say that it was too high. Yet every year we would meet or exceed those goals. Some of my sales people moved on to become phenomenal assets for other companies, and were able to hire and train their own successful sales forces. I can't help but feel at least partly responsible for those accomplishments."

Steve paused and looked concernedly towards Aaron.

"Is this boring?" He asked. "You don't look bored, but I always feel like I'm rambling on."

"You're not rambling at all," Aaron replied. "This is very interesting. Not only am I fascinated in what you're saying, there are some parts of your story that mirror my life very closely. I feel exactly the way you do about a commitment to lifelong learning. I've read the books you mentioned, and I've also trained a lot of good people who have gone on to train others using the lessons they learned from me." Aaron smiled. "I'm interested to hear how your life experiences led you to your current level of success. If your early life history was much like mine, then maybe you're about to give me the big clue I need to become as successful as you are today."

Steve laughed. "Alright then, I'll continue. But promise me that if I get boring you'll let me know."

"My snoring will be your signal to stop for a few minutes," Aaron said jokingly.

"Fair enough," Steve said, grinning.

# Chapter 7

"By the time I left the sales manager position, I wanted to try something new and challenging. My goal was to reach and help even more people than I'd been able to by working for just one company."

"Is that when you started giving seminars?" Aaron asked.

"It was exactly at that time," Steve acknowledged. "By that point in my career, I had experience standing in front of groups of people and speaking. They say that most people fear public speaking, but I loved it! I started offering sales training courses which slowly built up over the course of the next two years. I guess people liked my speeches, because the groups of attendees grew steadily. Soon I was standing in front of hundreds of people for hours at a time sharing my experience and knowledge."

"What topics did you talk about?" Aaron asked curiously.

"Well, at first I covered the basic skills of sales: prospecting, cold calling, negotiating, and so on. Everyone needs to work on the basics, so that's what I talked about. After the seminars, I would spend as much time as possible speaking with the attendees to try and find out what they needed to learn about the most to help them be successful. There are a ton of speakers out there, and I wanted to come up with a set of seminar topics that were unique in order to set myself apart from the competition. It didn't take long to get a general idea from seminar attendees that one much-needed topic was being inadequately covered. This topic was just waiting for someone to champion it. I had found my niche subject matter.

Steve paused. "Would you like to take a guess at what my focused niche was?"

"Sure," Aaron said. "Based on what I know about your business, and from what I've seen so far during my visits with the Gold Apples, I'm confident I can guess correctly."

"Guess away," Steve offered. "But you could be wrong. Maybe I tried another topic before finding this one."

Aaron grinned. "Actually I'm pretty confident about my guess. Was the topic 'customer service'?" Was the niche subject you decided upon Customer Service?"

"I guess I can't throw you off the trail so easily. You're absolutely right."

"Outstanding Customer Service!" Steve intoned formally. "It sounds so stuffy and official... and also so vague. The more I listened, the more I began to see that everyone was obsessed with excellent customer service, but they had no idea what it actually was. It's like wanting to ride a fabled creature....let's call it a Kurbmager. If you have no idea what a Kurbmager even looks like then you'll never be able to ride it will you? You could walk past one on your way to work every day and never realize what you're missing. This is the way it seemed to be for the topic of great customer service. People want 'it', but have no specific idea what 'it' is. Customers want to receive great customer service or they will buy elsewhere. Companies want to provide it in order to get more business. What I observed in reality, though, is that almost no one is delivering it. Outstanding customer service might as well be water in the desert. It's as precious and in demand as it is rare. If supply and demand means that the less there is of something, the more people want it, then ultra-rare customer service is definitely in high demand."

"Okay," Steve admitted, "I might be hitting this point over the head with a hammer, but I find it fascinating. I'm about to use an analogy to illustrate my point, and before I do let me just say that I'm a big fan of steak, hamburger, and hot dogs. I eat all three things and I don't want you to listen to my example and suddenly start to hate one or more of these foods."

"I'll do my best," Aaron said, a puzzled look on his face.

With a nod, Steve launched into his analogy.

"Exceptional customer service is like bringing a truckload of meat to a group of people. I inform them that the steak is the best cut and they should all try it. They sample some and agree with me that steak is best. Suddenly everyone demands the steak and they all eat it up like it's going out of style."

"But after a short amount of time, my supply runs out and I no longer have any steak to sell to the people. The population continues to demand steak and, even though I'm unable to provide them with steak, I still have a truck full of other perfectly good meat that I want to sell. So I talk to the people and show them the next best thing available: hamburger. I tell them that it's actually very similar in taste to steak, it just looks different. I assure them that it comes from the same animal and is very good. The people try the hamburger and all agree that it's not as good as the steak but, since this is all that's available, they buy it. Most people call the hamburger steak. A few individuals remind the others that this isn't steak and should be called by its proper name, hamburger. The majority of people say the name isn't really important, plus a new name could cause confusion. So the many ignore the few, and everyone continues to call their new meat of choice steak."

"Soon the hamburger runs out and I offer for sale the next best thing available: hot dogs. The people have developed a taste for meat by now, so they readily accept this new product. This new steak isn't as good as the last "steak" (most have forgotten the original steak altogether) but they all quickly adapt and accept the new alternative. At this point almost no one thinks to call this by a new name, and the few who insist on calling it hot dogs are largely ignored as troublemakers and conspiracy theorists."

"Customer service has gone the same route as the steak in my analogy." Steve concluded. "The customer service delivered today is primarily hot dogs. People are clamouring for better service, but most of the population doesn't even know what it is anymore."

"So, continuing with your analogy," said Aaron. "Even though everyone is eating hot dogs...if they ever taste real steak they might not know what to call it, but they can tell that it's much better than what they regularly get and respond accordingly to it."

"Exactly right," said Steve. "As for the people that are craving quality customer service, it's so rare that most people accept the poor service, not even realizing they could be getting better. Many people have had hot dogs so much, and so often, they no longer even miss the steak. You are absolutely right and my reasoning was the same; when they get steak, they notice the difference in quality and want more of the good stuff."

"My goal was to help people learn the lost and dying art of providing extraordinary customer service," Steve declared. "People might not know that they were not getting the best service, but if they started to receive it again they would instinctively appreciate it. The ability to provide exceptional customer service would give any individual or business instant and lasting success in the marketplace. I had found a void that needed to be filled."

"Alright, that makes sense to me." Aaron admitted. "So you had found your niche topic. How did you begin to train people on that? It sounds like a very interesting subject."

"Well, now that I had selected the topic." said Steve. "I began to compile what I'd learned from my experiences and tailor a seminar around it. I also started to pay more attention to customer service wherever I went. I thought I could use both the good and bad experiences to present as examples and lessons learned to my audiences. For my research I started to keep two journals. I kept a green notebook for the good customer service experiences, and red notebook for the, shall we say, unpleasant experiences."

"Guess which book I filled up first?" Steve asked."Truly surprise me and say the green notebook."

"I wish," Steve smiled wryly. "In fact, I hadn't filled the green one before I moved on to the second, third and even fourth red one! . I even started to write a bit larger in order to help that poor little green book out, but the amount of great customer service I experienced was as rare as I'd feared it would be."

"Seeing the lopsided state of customer service out there might have depressed some people, but it actually got me excited. I was confident that my idea was on the right track and so, I developed a course and began to promote it to all the people who had attended my previous sales seminars."

Steve paused and asked Aaron if he would like a drink. Aaron said yes to a bottle of water. Steve continued with his story as he went over to the bar.

"The people flocked to my new seminar." Steve said, pouring himself a mineral water. "At first it was mainly sales people who attended, but soon they began to bring their managers. Next the managers started bringing their customer service people. I was very pleased. My business had increased significantly, and I was truly helping people to improve the quality of their lives. I was also bringing on board a whole new set of customers by getting customer service people to attend. I soon expanded the seminar to offer three day weekend seminars with more hands on training. These events sold out quickly. Companies hired me to speak to their employees at their facilities. A book publisher contacted me to discuss writing a book on the topic of customer service. I was on top of the world."

Steve handed Aaron the bottle of water and then sat down.

"Then, after enjoying two years of phenomenal success," Steve said. "My excitement came crashing down in a fiery blaze of disappointment."

# Chapter 8

"What happened?" Aaron asked, surprised.

"Well," Steve said, looking as disappointed as if the event were actually happening to him now. "I had just given a seminar and was mingling with the attendees, as was my routine. I happened to recognize a couple of people and thanked them for coming again. Then I began to realize that I was recognizing more than just a couple of people...there were a lot. I began to seek them out in the crowd. I would ask them if they had brought a new friend to the seminar to hear my message. I was disheartened to hear most of the people report that no, they didn't bring anyone, they just had such a great time that they wanted to come again. Some even said that this was their third or fourth time coming to this exact same seminar. I was crushed."

Aaron was perplexed. "Why were you crushed? I would think that ten people coming back to see you three times is a compliment. They were happy too, right? So you made more money selling your product to happy customers. I can tell by your face that I'm missing something, so tell me what it is."

"I wanted this seminar to be so understandable and concise that people would only need to come and see it once. They would be so clear on the topic, so hyped up and ready to go, that they wouldn't need to come back. They could get out into the world to provide outstanding customer service and help others to do the same. It appeared that wasn't happening though. I'd put hundreds of hours of effort and delivery into a program that wasn't working as I had planned."

"So standing there at that seminar, meeting with dozens of re-peat attendees, I felt crushed." Steve paused, a clever grin appeared on his face. "For about thirty seconds."

It was Aaron's turn to grin. "That's it? Crushed for only thirty seconds? That's an excellent recovery time!"

"Well what can I say?" Steve grinned back. "I've worked hard over the years to be a positive guy. Two people can see an event hap-pen and one sees it as bad while the other sees it as good. I learned early on that the human brain only sees what it looks for. So when something bad happens in my life, I allow myself thirty seconds to wallow in the bad and then, I look for the good."

"Has that strategy worked well for you?" Aaron asked.

Steve laughed. "The answer to that question depends on when you ask it. Ask me within thirty seconds of a bad event in my life, and I would tell you that it doesn't work well at all and it's a mis-erable rule which I should abolish. If you ask me at any other time, then I'll tell you it's a great exercise that's given me the positive en-ergy I need to learn from my mistakes and move on towards suc-cess. Final answer though is that it works great!"

"So after thirty seconds of being crushed, what did you decide to do, in a positive way, about the situation?" Aaron asked.

"Well, I decided to ask myself a bunch of questions over the next few days," Steve answered. "I asked myself what the purpose for these seminars was. What was I really trying to accomplish, and was this the best way to do it? I wanted to de-mystify customer ser-vice. There are many people who give great customer service but they don't know how or why they do it. Conversely, there are many more people who give horrible customer service and they also have no clue why or how they do it. I believed I had come up with a simple set of rules that, if adhered to, would consistently result in the delivery of great customer service."

"The Gold Apple rules of customer service!" Aaron piped up.

"Exactly," Steve confirmed, "although they weren't called that at the time. They were just called the rules of customer service."

"So, in your opinion, why were the seminars ineffective at conveying these rules?" asked Aaron.

"I realized the seminar was a fine way to convey the rules," Steve admitted. "But what I really wanted was not to just stand in front of a group and present an idea. I wanted to start a movement."

"A movement," Aaron echoed thoughtfully. "I think I'm beginning to see your big picture idea, Steve, and I agree with you. Your seminar wasn't the best way to start a movement."

"Really?" Steve was interested in hearing Aaron's opinion on this. "Why not?

"Because even a large group of people won't contain enough individuals who are able to take the information from your seminar and integrate it into their daily lives, which is what you need before you can call it a movement."

"What makes you think that rooms full of people paying to attend a seminar won't adopt the information they came to learn?" Steve asked curiously.

Aaron put his thoughts in order, and then voiced his opinion. "There are some really sharp and motivated people that go to seminars. People like you, and me, who are committed to hearing something new and then incorporating it into their lives. The majority of people that go to seminars aren't like that, though. Most people attend seminars where they listen attentively, take notes and get all fired up. Then they go home and a week later, almost none of them are doing anything that they learned. Often they couldn't even tell you what they really experienced."

"Why do you think that is?" Steve queried.

"I think there are two reasons. One is that there's simply too much information to absorb. Even the sharpest person will only be able to adopt a few key points from a seminar."

"The second reason," Aaron shrugged, "is that most people don't get it."

Steve bit the inside of his cheek to avoid smiling, not wanting to give away how pleased he was with his latest Platinum selection. "Most people don't get what?" He asked.

Aaron chuckled. "You name it, and they don't get it."

Aaron hesitated for a moment, and then decided to continue. "There are two types of people in the world. Let's pretend that both of them witness the same event. The first person, let's call them 'Type U', observes the event and, thinking of themselves as merely a bystander, they walk by and quickly forget about what they have just seen. They never give it another thought. The second type of person, 'Type I' sees the event and, even though it doesn't directly affect them at the time, they don't forget about it. Type I wonders if they can learn anything from the event and they often do take away a lesson and apply to their own life. The second person, the Type I, is the lifelong learner. Type U is not. I wish that the majority of people were like the second one, but the simple truth is that most people are Type U, non learners."

"I'm with you...but you haven't answered my question yet. Why, in your view, don't people get it?"

"Because they don't realize that there's anything to get. They see nothing worth learning from the experience. The Type U, non-learner doesn't find out why because they don't care. Either it doesn't occur to them that there is a why, or else they're not concerned with finding an answer so they don't bother to look for one. It might sound cruel, but it isn't meant to be. There's nothing wrong with being either a Type U, or Type I person; each personality has its own strengths and weaknesses. I'm just saying that if a person sees a door and isn't curious about what's behind it, then they'll never ask anyone "Hey what's behind that door?"

"I agree with you," Steve was nodding. "I think your explanation was very sound. You didn't sound cruel at all."

"I explain it like this," Steve said. He held up his glass of mineral water. "I can attempt to physically transform this glass of mineral water into a can of soda. I can learn all about the differences between soda and mineral water. I can become a chemist in order to better comprehend the chemical breakdowns and properties of each. I can even spend millions of dollars hiring other people to make a team and buy a factory to work at it. But no matter how much time I spend, or how hard I try, I will never be able to make this glass of mineral water change into a can of soda. It's the same with "getting it" on the level we are talking about, I think. Either you have the ability to, or you don't."

Aaron laughed. "That illustrates the point perfectly, I think."

Steve smiled. "Thanks. Some people tell me it's too ridiculous to accept, so I've come up with another example. Let's say I have a canvas painted in red and blue colors. I show it to someone who only sees the world in black and white, they don't have the cones and rods in their eyes to see colour. No matter how skilled I am at teaching, speaking, or communicating, the person in front of me will never see the red and blue on the canvas."

"I like that." Aaron said appreciatively. "You were giving a seminar on colour when so many of the people attending were color blind. No matter how many times they attended they would never be able to see the actual colors."

"Not enough of the right people were attending my seminar." Steve agreed. "It explains why the seminar was not the way to start my movement. I wasn't reaching enough of my targeted demographic. Oh sure some of the right ones were in there, but not enough."

"So you decided to stop giving the customer service seminars," Aaron concluded.

"Not at all," Steve said.

"But," Aaron looked confused, "You said the seminars were not the best way to get the movement started."

Steve looked at Aaron as he sipped his mineral water. "I led you to make an assumption. They are so bad I should really put them into one of my rules of customer service."

Aaron grinned sheepishly.

"Don't pay any attention to me," Steve said with a smile. "I try to make these talks entertaining for me too. I led you right into that assumption. I did keep doing the seminars. I simply changed what I wanted to get out of them, and then modified the seminar accordingly."

"After talking to many attendees, I also realized that there are degrees of everything...including colour-blindness, to use my example. Everyone who attends seminars is a person who wants to improve themselves to some extent. Not many non-learners spend their hard-earned money and precious free time to attend seminars. I think it's safe to say that almost all of the people who attend seminars are lifelong learners to some degree, Type I people with the best of intentions. After meeting and talking with so many of these people, I can also tell you that even though many of them will not absorb the entire message of the seminar, they still take away some good practical information that they go on to use to enrich their lives."

Aaron considered this. "So you're saying that some people might get one point and apply it, while others might only be able to maintain their motivation from the seminar for a few days or weeks. Even though all don't incorporate something from your seminar into their lives permanently, they are still affected by the message for some length of time. So it's worth it to them to have attended?"

"That's what I've seen to be true," said Steve. "Particularly if the topic is not that person's personal passion. I know for a fact that there are courses I've taken and found interesting, but because it wasn't my passion I only learned a little bit, needing to revisit the information and even take the seminar or read the book again to refresh my mind with the information."

Aaron nodded thoughtfully, realizing that this was also the case for some of the things he had learned in his life. "Was my comment about people not getting it too harsh then?" He asked.

"Not in the least." Steve shook his head. "I agree one hundred percent with your observation about learners and non-learners.

"The other thing to remember is that I wanted something as a result of the seminars that the attendees had no interest in at all. I decided to continue the seminars. The people attending could continue to come for their reasons, and I would pursue my reasons for having the seminars in a better way."

"It was at this point in time," Steve declared, "that I came up with the idea of the Gold Apples."

# Chapter 9

"Aha!" Aaron proclaimed, "The birth of a movement!"

Steve looked at Aaron with an amused look. "Yes indeed. Many times when I would talk to people and ask them how they planned to go back to their lives and incorporate what I'd taught, they would express concern about how their co-workers might react. Many would say that my ideas had great potential but they felt they'd go back to their office and have one or two negative people sabotage their good intentions. My reply to this common concern soon became, "Well you're going back with good to combat their bad. If one bad apple can spoil the bunch, what can a gold apple do?""

"Sounds catchy," Aaron said with a sparkle in his eye.

"Well it does now," laughed Steve. "I must have said that to over 300 people before it occurred to me that I could put it on a business card."

"So," Steve continued, "instead of training people to become excellent at customer service, I decided to find people who were already naturals at providing great customer service. Many of them displayed the raw instinct that would enable them to become even better at customer service, once they learned my rules and put them into practice," Steve raised his now empty glass. "I started looking for glasses of mineral water instead of trying to make them from cans of soda."

"Sounds like good sense," said Aaron. "How did you use the seminars to do this?"

"I had the gold apple cards, which you've become familiar with, printed up. Then I took the cards and, wherever I went, if I encountered someone who displayed the qualities of a "natural" I would hand them a card. The address on the back would be for the hotel of my upcoming seminar. The gold apple card got them free admission into the seminar."

"So you would do a seminar with regular attendees who paid to come learn?" Aaron asked for clarification. "Then, the Gold Apples would be invited for free?"

"Exactly," Steve confirmed. "I was also on the lookout for new attendees who were undiscovered Gold Apples. During the seminar I would attempt to pick them out of the crowd. I got pretty good at it over time. You've already learned that groups of people share common traits and the Gold Apples are a definite identifiable group. If I felt that an attendee was a Gold Apple I would stop whatever I was doing during the seminar, walk up to them, and hand them a gold apple card. At the conclusion of my seminars, I would invite everyone with a gold apple card to come join me for a free meal at one of the hotel ballrooms."

"How did your strategy work out?" Aaron asked.

"Like a charm." Steve replied smiling. "Over a short period of time I began to compile a group of Gold Apples in each city where I would host a seminar. I then developed a new seminar for "Gold Apples only" where I taught the rules in more detail with much more interaction between me and the Gold Apples. This Gold Apple seminar was free as well."

"Free?" Aaron was intrigued. "I think I can guess the answer, but business people would say you were losing money by offering your time for free. Why do that?"

Steve nodded. "The regular seminars were bringing in enough dollars, and so more money wasn't really my concern. Finding and training Gold Apples was my real passion, changing the quality of customer service for everyone. I didn't need to charge the Gold Apples for coming to learn. The regular seminar brought enough people to the hotels that I was able to negotiate an extra small meeting room at minimal cost. The meal wasn't very expensive. Most important to me, I was starting to get together the people that could make a difference to the world. I wanted to not just tell them about great customer service, I wanted to show them great customer service as well! A free training seminar with some perks made them feel as special as they were."

"I've wanted to ask this since day one." Aaron leaned forward curiously. "Why call them Gold Apples? I've always heard the phrase "golden apple". Why not call them that?

"Well that's a question I hear a lot. The answer is not that exciting, but here it is. When I think of the word golden I picture something that's gold coloured, but not solid gold. I looked the word up in the dictionary and the definition was something gold coloured, or something mostly made of gold. It was close, but my picture was an apple of pure gold. So I decided to call them Gold Apples."

"That makes sense to me." Aaron nodded. "So what did you plan to do with your Gold Apples? Train them and then what?"

"Yeah," Steve nodded. "That was my same question right about that time in the process. What did I plan to do with them? I'd been thinking about a couple of possibilities but, as luck would have it, the best answer came from some of the Gold Apples themselves."

"Some of these newly discovered Gold Apples owned their own businesses. Six of them asked if I would get together privately with them for a meeting. They were from different cities but were all willing to fly to one place to meet. Apparently, they had a business proposition for me. I was intrigued, thinking maybe they wanted me to do a seminar for local groups that they might each belong to, so I agreed to meet with them."

"At the meeting they asked me what my plans were for the Gold Apples. I said that my major goal was for each Gold Apple to master the rules I had identified for extraordinary customer service, and then go to the places where they worked and effect change, making those businesses and their co-workers all more successful by training others around them to also give great customer service. The phrase on the gold apple card was the goal, for one gold apple in an establishment to turn the surrounding people into gold also."

"The six business owners acknowledged that my idea was a good one. But they were concerned that progress might be slow and that in many places such a big change would never take off. I agreed, having the same concerns myself, and asked them genuinely if they had a better idea. The six smiled at one another and then showed me their idea. After they had gone through the presentation and I had asked my customary exhaustive amount of questions, I sat there, more excited than I can remember ever having been about the Gold Apples before."

"What was their idea?" Aaron asked, leaning forward with full attention.

"The six business owners," Steve continued, "had interpreted the message on my card as well, but in a different way. They felt that Gold Apples could indeed affect change and show the world the power of excellent customer service, but not as individual people. Their idea was for individual businesses to be made up entirely of Gold Apples."

"Absolutely, "Aaron agreed. "An individual could affect change, but it would be small and grow slowly. Then there would be the risk that others would not recognize the reason for the success—-great customer service—and give the credit to something else."

"Precisely," said Steve. "But a business providing Gold Apple service could quickly rise to the top of its industry. A restaurant, for instance, could become very successful and everyone would know about both the success and the reason for it."

"The Gold Apple businesses and I began to come up with the specifics of the strategy. From that point on, they agreed to hire only gold apple card holders as employees. They also agreed to review their current staff, and keep only Gold Apples. As you can imagine, there was a big hiring of Gold Apples initially."

"As well a large amount of pink slips handed out at the six Gold Apple businesses," Aaron raised an eyebrow.

"That's right." Steve nodded. "Do you think that's bad?"

"I'm not sure." Aaron looked genuinely torn between feeling bad for the people who were fired and confident that it was a good decision for the businesses.

"Walk into almost any business today," Steve challenged. "Inform them that you have a person ready and willing to work for them. A new person, who's better than anyone they currently employ. Regardless of whether that business is hiring or not, if they believe your claim then most will jump at the chance to get a new excellent employee. I've done this numerous times and most do jump at the chance... because the old adage is true; good people are hard to find. Great people are next to impossible to find."

Aaron agreed, nodding his head.

"If you want to build a Gold Apple business, then it's crucial to have an entire Gold Apple staff. The Gold Apples who owned business (or 'Business Gold Apples' as I've come to call them), agreed on this from the beginning. Each of them was committed to staffing their establishments in the proper way. I can assure you though, not one existing employee who did a great job was fired."

"So it was that simple." Aaron said. "Hire a solid staff of Gold Apples and watch the success happen?"

Steve grinned. "Actually, it was almost that simple, yeah. My contribution was finding and training the Gold Apples. Then I'd send them to the business that could use their skills. Once the teams were in place, the business Gold Apple and I would plan how to specifically grow their business. We trained the new employees in the mechanics of their new jobs and then let them loose. It didn't take long for the Gold Apple businesses to begin to rise to the top of their respective industries."

"What do you mean by mechanics?" Aaron asked.

"By mechanics of a business I mean the procedural way that tasks are performed, the functions that make the business tick." Steve explained. "At the restaurant, some examples would be the operation of the computer ordering system, the organization of the kitchen, the procedures for making meals and so on. At the shoe store it was the technical stuff like what types of shoes they sold, how to select a shoe for a customer, what brand was better for a wide foot vs. narrow, stuff like that. Mechanics are the things that you can teach anyone, given the time and energy. The assets that the Gold Apples brought to the businesses were what I call the intangibles."

"The skills that couldn't be trained?" Aaron ventured to guess.

"Right," Steve confirmed, "the things that made them Gold Apples at customer service. I could instruct a person to do everything possible to make a customer happy. A regular person might know to do one or two steps of a minimum ten-step process. A Gold Apple would instinctively know all ten steps, and likely add two or three of their own to enhance the experience even further. That's the stuff you can't train. It's also the most important aspect of success to a business."

"Your contribution to find, place, and train the Gold Apples sounds like it would take up most of your time." Aaron commented. "Were you able to still do as many seminars?"

"It demanded a huge amount of my time." Steve admitted. "The seminars got put on hold, although I actually didn't mind too much. I'd been doing the seminars for a number of years. I figured I could take a break and come back to it later on. From a monetary standpoint, the seminar income had left me well off. The business Gold Apples brought me in as partners to each of their business as well, and as the success of each business grew so did my bank statement."

Aaron laughed out loud. "Are you kidding me? I've been to three of the original Gold Apple Businesses right?"

Steve nodded.

"Well then, I guess you're doing very well from a monetary standpoint." Aaron shook his head in wonder. "Each of those places is a gold mine if I ever saw one. You could retire right?"

It was Steve's turn to shake his head. "I could, I guess. But why retire when you're doing something you love to do? This has become a movement just like I envisioned. Even though it's bigger than I could have imagined in such a short time, I think it's growth is about to explode, and I want to be around to see it happen."

"From what you've told me so far, the seminars were a great way to find Gold Apple employees. Since you were no longer doing them, how did you find enough Gold Apples for the businesses?"

"I had a large base of Gold Apples discovered from previous seminars already." Steve said. "I also had a lot of gold apple cards made up. My six business Gold Apple colleagues and I hit the streets looking to fill the remaining spots that were open, after we exhausted our existing data base. We would find a person who fit our criteria and then give them a card. Then as the cards led the new Gold Apples to us, we would ask successful candidates if they had any friends who had the same values and skill sets as they did. Usually each Gold Apple would know one or two people similar to them. That's how we did it. Some of the businesses didn't require many staff people, Jake's Shoes for example. Other businesses like the restaurant did."

"Once each business was ready to go," Steve continued, "they would relaunch and our project began. If anyone had doubts about the power of excellent customer service prior to that, they were quickly answered. Each Gold Apple facility quickly began to see an increase in repeat business, as well as in volume of sales and customer satisfaction. We also looked for some marketing help, which we naturally found in the form of one particular Gold Apple, and over the past five years the Gold Apple businesses have been carving out a top spot whenever, and wherever they open. The six businesses have grown to thirteen, and we're able and willing to continue adding more as fast as we can find them."

"By grow, do you mean start franchises?" Aaron asked.

"Not really, no." Steve shook his head. "Al wanted to try franchising with the gas stations, so we're going ahead with that slowly. Franchising is considered a different project though. A close eye is being kept on Al's experiment because often when a company grows, customer service is the first thing to suffer – and that would destroy our primary purpose. Jenn dropped into Al's lap and we felt that if anyone would be up to the considerable challenges involved with a franchise, it would be her. So we're trying it out—with success so far, I'd like to add. We want to keep the other businesses unique at the moment."

"Like in Europe," Aaron nodded.

"What do you mean?" Steve asked.

"In Europe, you'll find many restaurants with excellent food and customer service," Aaron explained. "There's a large volume of quaint, unique places. I think they are successful, in part, because they are unique. If you had a corner bistro named Jean-Paul's try to franchise, it would ruin the whole idea."

"That's one good reason to stay small," Steve admitted, "But not the main one in our case. The main reason is availability of Gold Apples. If it takes sixty Gold Apple restaurant workers to run one successful restaurant, and you want to open up three more restaurants of the same name and style, we simply haven't been able to find another 180 Gold Apple chefs, servers and hospitality staff yet. And opening a Gold Apple restaurant without enough Gold Apples to staff it is simply unthinkable."

"Isn't any Gold Apple good enough to put into a restaurant?" Aaron asked.

"I see your point. But I've realized that there are many types of Gold Apples." Steve said. "While there are qualities that make all Gold Apples similar, it turns out that many Gold Apples are specific to their chosen profession. I know of a dishwasher, for example, who is one of the best I have ever seen. She displays all the Gold Apple qualities and traits, but she has no desire to try to be a president of a large company. If I offer a Gold Apple accountant the open position for a waiter at our new restaurant, while I'm sure he could do a great job if he took the position, it's highly unlikely that he will leave his accounting firm to wait tables."

"Ah, ok I understand." Aaron nodded. "The good thing is that every walk of life and every job out there can benefit from Gold Apples though."

"Exactly," Steve agreed.

"Are you saying you think it's impossible to find that many restaurant Gold Apples then?" Aaron asked.

"Oh, it's definitely possible." Steve said with a nod of his head. "But using our methods, and also being so involved to open the new stores has kept the pace of growing steady but slow. This isn't something you can go out and do in three months. The Gold Apples are out there," Steve said positively. "We just need to keep finding them. One other factor that's seriously keeping growth at its current pace is the scarcity of what I call the business Gold Apple. A business Gold Apple is a business owner who wants to take his business and turn it from something good, into something great."

"There are hundreds of thousands of businesses like that out there," Aaron said confidently. "I would guess that almost every business in existence wants to be great and successful."

Steve laughed. "That's what I thought too and let me assure you that line of thought is a perfect example of how assumptions are bad. Looking for business Gold Apple candidates is an excellent way to see Show vs. Tell and Assumptions are Bad in reality. I've visited numerous businesses and met with countless presidents and owners. Almost all of these people *tell* me that they want to be great, but they *show* me they really don't."

"Well, I believe you," Aaron said with a doubtful look. "But I'm amazed to hear that."

"Wanting to be great is easy," Steve said. "Yet if you own a business that's already profitable, making the necessary moves that we recommend towards greatness can be difficult. The average business is not often willing to take the steps required. The truth is that most good businesses are content to be good, and the other businesses wouldn't know how to get better if the solution came to their door and told them."

"Let me give you an example." Steve offered. "You're a business owner of a successful ten-year old company. You've grown from $100,000 in sales your first year, with one employee, to current sales of two million dollars last year with fourteen employees."

"Sounds pretty good," Aaron admitted.

"It is," Steve acknowledged, "but say I come to you and tell you that I have a sure way for you to quadruple your sales in the next three to five years, as well as expand your staff from fourteen to forty while increasing your profit by at least fifteen to twenty percent. Are you interested?" Steve asked.

"Absolutely!" Aaron exclaimed.

Steve nodded. "Great. I meet with your employees and then I inform you that the first step you will need to take is to fire twelve of your current fourteen employees."

"Why fire so many?" Aaron asked, looking concerned.

"We need to fire so many," Steve explained, "because twelve of them don't do the job that you hired them to do. They don't even come close to doing a good job. In fact, having them on the payroll is causing you to lose money. If you had better people filling those positions, you would likely have sold four to six million dollars worth of product last year instead of only two!"

"Wow is that true?" Aaron asked in disbelief.

"From my experiences, it's absolutely true," Steve replied. "And that's the point where usually the meeting ends, and the business who has told me they want to grow, shows me that they really don't."

"Why does the meeting end at that point?"

"Because," Steve sighed, "the owner or president gets offended. They and their people have worked very hard to find and train these people. Sure these employees aren't perfect, they admit, but they are pretty good employees. I can give you hundreds of reasons and excuses, which I have heard so many times, but in the end that's all they are. Reasons and excuses for failure. Most businesses say they want to get better, but they aren't willing to actually do what's required to succeed."

"Then, the now hostile owner," Steve said, "asks me who I am anyway. What makes me think I have knowledge to create a more successful business than he could? What are my credentials? Where did I get my MBA? What successes do I have to walk into his office and make such claims?"

"It's at that point that I smile politely, thank him for his time, and leave his office."

"Why not tell him who you are?" Aaron asked. "Give him your credentials. List the businesses you have helped."

"I don't waste my time," Steve answered calmly, "because that information won't help him. I don't want to waste my time with a can of soda. I'm looking for this." Steve held up his glass of mineral water.

"What kind of reaction would a business Gold Apple have to your diagnosis?"

"A business Gold Apple would not become hostile or offended. I'm tactful in my observations and claims. I know how to convey sensitive information without insulting people. A business Gold Apple would be interested in my opinion and ask some good questions to get more detail out of me. Gold Apples don't focus on problems, they focus on solutions. When you're focused on the solution you don't worry about blaming others, or attack those around you. If I talk to a business owner and they're interested in finding a solution, maybe not mine, but I can sense from their reactions that they have a keen desire to make things better, then I know I've found someone with potential." Steve got up to refill his and Aaron's glasses. "There's still the chance that a positive person can turn negative, and so I talk with these potential business Gold Apples either until the conversation is over and I'm certain they're a Gold Apple candidate, or until they revert back to their usual way of breathing and turn negative again. The search is slow, but I can't think of a better way to do it faster. I think in this case the old idiom is true, you can't rush perfection."

"What did you just mean?" Aaron was curious to know. "When you said that they revert back to their way of breathing and turn negative again?"

"That's right. How you Breathe is another Gold Apple philosophy of mine." Steve looked at his watch, and then asked. "I'm hungry, how about you?"

It was Aaron's turn to look at his watch, it read 7 p.m. He had been talking with Steve for three hours now.

Aaron nodded affirmatively. "I'm hungry. Would you like to continue our talk on another day?"

Steve smiled. "Not really. If you can hang in a bit longer, I'd like to continue our discussion. It will end with some interesting stuff for you to consider, I can assure you. I was thinking of treating you to dinner where we can continue to discuss matters."

"Sure, that sounds good to me," Aaron complied. "Where did you have in mind?"

"Well, I know you were there the other day for lunch, but Customer's Paradise makes great dinner also, if you'd like to check it out."

"That would be great!" Aaron said. "Can we get in without a reservation though? I thought they are booked up months in advance?"

Steve acknowledged that they were. "But I have a standing reservation with them even though I don't eat there every night. The nights I don't call them to say I'll be dining, they simply call the waiting list and fill my spot with some lucky group. It's one of the perks of being a part owner."

"Well then I'm ready to go when you are." Aaron said, rising to his feet.

"Great, I'll tell you about my breathing philosophy when we get there."

# Chapter 10

The two of them drove to the restaurant in Steve's car, making small talk during the drive. By the time they got to the restaurant each person knew a lot more about the other. More often than not, the two would chuckle at how similar their backgrounds were. Both were small town country boys who had grown up and made their way to the city to find better opportunities for success. Even their jobs and educational backgrounds were similar for the most part. They seemed to be getting along on a personal level very well.

They arrived at Customer's Paradise and were immediately ushered to a table that had a small "reserved" sign on it. Everyone knew Steve and those who weren't too busy made sure to stop by and say hello. Steve introduced Aaron to each one and identified him as a new Platinum Gold Apple. Everyone he met welcomed him to the Gold Apple family. .

A half hour after being seated, the commotion of Steve's arrival had settled down, and the two men were once again left to themselves to enjoy their glasses of wine and get back down to discussion.

"How you breathe," Steve picked up right where he had left off at the office, "is one of my favorite analogies— I think because it explains why some people seem to 'get it' as you said earlier. Specifically, some get it almost right away, while others never get it no matter how much time and energy you put into helping them.

"Imagine swimming in a lake." Steve began. "As you float above the surface, you breathe air. It's effortless for you to breathe air above the water, because that's what you were made to do. That's how you breathe."

"Now below the surface of the lake you spy a fish. It breathes in a very different way, right?"

Aaron nodded. "Entirely different. The fish takes in oxygen from the water using gills instead of lungs."

"That's right," agreed Steve. "A fish's anatomy enables it to breathe under water."

"So the fish and you breathe differently. Now let me ask you this. Can you go under water and breathe there? Or can the fish leave the water and breathe on land?"

"No," Aaron replied. "The fish can be taken out of the water for a short time, and I can go underwater for a short time, but neither of us can breathe in the wrong environment. So after a few minutes, both of us would die."

"Correct," Steve nodded. "Both of you could hold your breath for a certain amount of time, but eventually you would have to go back to your own way of breathing. You would swim to the surface for air, and the fish would struggle to get back into the water for the same precious commodity. "

"I think it's important to mention," Steve concluded his analogy, "That the way someone breathes can be used to explain any skill or trait. We're going to talk about providing great customer service, but you could easily apply the breathing analogy to a person's ability to do math, or to play a sport, or to do anything. Everyone has the ability to be good at something. Just because a person doesn't breathe great customer service doesn't mean they don't breathe excellence in some other skill or aspect of their lives."

"I can see your point," Aaron nodded. "Ross talked about the ability to write music when I met him. I don't breathe well at making songs. Actually I drown almost immediately."

Steve laughed.

"Good. Now let's apply this breathing analogy to providing great customer service. I select two people and give them both an intense three-week training program on how to deliver excellent customer service. Each person receives the same classroom teaching, stories, and books to read on the subject, practical examples to learn from, and so on. I would expect both of them to be either very good at customer service or both very bad, depending on the quality of training I had given them. Instead of this occurring, however, something very different and strange happens.

"One of the people is excellent! She gives customer service like a pro. She's able to take all the information that was given to her during training and absorb it like a sponge, using it to help her provide exemplary customer service time after consistent time. There's no challenge I can throw at her that doesn't result in the delivery of great customer service!"

"The second person, on the other hand, struggles constantly to give good customer service. She starts off pretty good, giving good customer service for the first few tries. Then she seems to fall off the wagon. Her customer service is terrible. Even giving her the easiest of challenges results in such poor customer service that often, the customer vows never to return. Every once in a while this struggling person puts on a burst and seems to do an adequate job of it, but she is never able to do as good as the first person did."

"What's happened," Steve concluded, "is that these two people breathe differently when it comes to delivering customer service. The first person breathes excellent customer service. They can do it with what looks to be no effort at all, and they can do it for as long as we need them to. If you were to ask this person how they are able to be so good at this, they will likely reply, "it's not difficult, I'm just using common sense."

"The second person can 'hold their breath' and provide satisfactory customer service...for a short time. But eventually that person will have to swim for the top of the water and begin to breathe naturally again for themselves, at which point good customer service disappears. Ask this person what's wrong and they'll reply, "This is ridiculous and stupid. No one can be expected to do any better than I'm doing, I need better training and more time to practice.""

"That," Aaron said slowly, "is a very interesting analogy."

"Do you like it?" Steve asked.

"I really do!" Aaron said. "Am I correct to guess that the "naturals" who breathe customer service are Gold Apples?"

"Yes, that's exactly right." Steve said.

"But how can you be certain you've found a Gold Apple and not simply someone who's really good at holding their breath?" Aaron was sure Steve had an answer to this question, and he was curious to hear it.

"In reality, it's quite easy to tell the two apart," Steve replied. "If you spend enough time with a person, you'll get an idea of which type of individual they are. One or two experiences with a person usually doesn't give you enough information because there are some people out there who have become very, very good at holding their breath."

"Let me give you an example of someone who doesn't 'breathe' customer service, but can still be good, even excellent at it...for short periods of time."

"Let's imagine a young man in the customer service field, let's call him Dwight. Young Dwight got into the customer service industry quite by accident. This field of business didn't really interest him, but he stayed anyway. He wanted to make as much money as he could at his current job, so he decided to take a few of the free customer service courses offered by his employer. Being a good student, Dwight quickly mastered some of the tricks and tips provided to him from these classes and he went on to be a great customer service representative for his employer. From 8:00 a.m. to 5:00 p.m. every day, Dwight would answer incoming calls and in a very capable and helpful manner provide good customer service to his clients. Many people even started to request Dwight by name when they called in. Dwight did very well at his job, excelling higher than most of his co-workers. He even became a manager and started to train and oversee other co-workers. But Dwight was holding his breath when it came to customer service. He was able to hold his breath much longer than most, and during that time provide good customer service. He isn't the Gold Apple I'm searching for, though."

"In what ways did he hold his breath?" Aaron asked.

"I'm glad you asked," Steve smiled. "Dwight gave good customer service to the people that called him on the phone, and that's the only time he gave good customer service. He wasn't considerate of his co-workers, friends, or family because he didn't consider them to be his customers. When he would go to a department store, Dwight wasn't so pleasant to the customer service people helping him; he wasn't a good customer. On the weekends he would go to the bar with friends and not tip the bartender when it was his turn to buy drinks. He would get a ride with his friends and never thank them or offer to pay for gas. When living his day-to-day life, Dwight was oblivious of others, not interested in people unless he wanted something from them. He was selfish, inconsiderate and often politely rude when he breathed naturally. Do you see what I mean when I say he was holding his breath at work?"

"Yes, I see what you mean now," Aaron agreed. "If he breathed excellent customer service then Dwight would view everyone he interacted with as a customer. He would always do his best to provide good experiences both for himself and for the other person involved, not just when he was 'on the clock.'"

"That's precisely right," said Steve. "Gold Apples always stand out. A guy like Dwight has it turned off much more than he has it turned on, and it doesn't bother him that the majority of his average day is spent being selfish and inconsiderate of others. Great customer service isn't part of his character; it's not how he breathes. Dwight's an excellent example of someone who gives great customer service to one group of people and for short periods of time. I would be able to ascertain that Dwight wasn't a Gold Apple very quickly. Taking him out for lunch and watching how he interacts with strangers would likely be enough for me to see him actually "breathing".

"So that's what you look for in a Gold Apple?" Aaron asked. "If they have it in their character, if they breathe customer service all the time then that's how you know they are a Gold Apple?"

"That's right," Steve acknowledged. "If a person primarily displays the three rules no matter where they are, or what they are doing, then he or she is a Gold Apple. Dwight turned his use of the rules on for work, and then at 5:00 p.m. he turned them off and went back to being a selfish person who didn't care about others, wasn't easy to do business with, and stopped asking questions with lots of assuming thrown into the mix. Dwight had learned to be a good, even great employee. Many companies would be glad to have him because he's better at providing customer service than most of the other people out there. Dwight was a learner, so he was able to go out and learn customer service so he could make more money. He's still not a Gold Apple. "

"And he never will be?"

"No, unfortunately he won't."

"What about me?" Aaron was suddenly curious. "You said one interaction with a person is not enough to truly know if they're a Gold Apple or not. I think I only met you the one time, so how did you feel comfortable enough to give me not just a gold apple card, but a platinum apple card?"

Steve smiled slyly. "In the customer service world, you were noticed by the owner of this restaurant, Ross, who mentioned you to me. I then made some inquiries and sent a few Gold Apples to buy from you. Each one would rate you on your customer service; you always got great marks by the way. Before I handed you the Platinum card you had been exposed to so many Gold Apples, that I was very sure you fit our criteria. After my impressive experience with you I decided you were Platinum.

"And trust me," Steve winked, "you're Platinum."

The meal arrived, and the men decided to halt their discussion about Gold Apples until the meal was finished. During the meal, Ross stopped at their table to greet the two men and make certain that everything was enjoyable. Steve brought Ross up to speed on where the discussion had led so far with Aaron. Ross listened attentively, nodding and smiling at certain points. He observed out loud that Aaron seemed to be asking some excellent questions to unravel the Gold Apples movement so far.

"You still don't know about platinum apple card holders, or the special opportunity they are presented with?" Ross asked pleasantly.

"No, not yet," Aaron shrugged. "I figured Steve would get to it in his own time."

Steve chuckled. "Ross knows that now is that time. That's why he stuck his head out here, to come and listen in, if my guess is right."

Ross let out a laugh. "You know I enjoy the Platinum talk, Steve." He looked sideways at Aaron, "Platinum gold apples are rare, so yes I enjoy being part of it when I can. If Steve lets me stay it will only be the third time I've heard the explanation given to the actual card holder."

"How many Platinum apple card holders have there been?" Aaron asked, his interest level rising at hearing that platinum apple card holders were rarer than he would have guessed.

"Over the past six years we've discovered approximately 820 gold apple card holders." Steve recited from memory. "There are thirteen Gold Apple businesses at the moment. That means a business owned by a Gold Apple who is committed to fully staff his organization with Gold Apples only." Steve paused with an amused expression on his face to look at Ross. "That also means there are at least thirteen newly made multi millionaires as a result of Gold Apples."

"At least," Ross grinned broadly, obviously one of the millionaires in question.

"To answer your question, Aaron," Steve concluded. "Including you, six people have been given the platinum apple card."

# Chapter 11

"Only six Platinum cards have been given out." Aaron considered this fact. "I would have guessed there were more. I thought that a Platinum was..." he paused. "Well I guess I never really thought about it." Aaron admitted.

"It's because you don't accept praise well," Steve said. "You think that you don't really do anything special, so why would you be given a rare card? Does that sound about right?" He asked.

"Yeah, it does." Aaron admitted. "I guess the $10,000 value of the card should have tipped me off that it wasn't so common. I figured you were likely an eccentric millionaire who could afford such a tip."

"Well I likely am both of those things." Steve laughed. "I still don't give out the Platinum card often, though. Let me explain what it is and why I started handing it out."

"Please do." Aaron said.

Ross had brought coffee and dessert. He joined them at their table now, waiting for Steve to begin his explanation.

"My experiences with the business Gold Apples," Steve began, "taught me that there are other likeminded people out there who not only share in my vision of the Gold Apple movement, but they can also see strategies that I don't."

He nodded to Ross appreciatively. "If this ruffian and his five friends hadn't convinced me to form Gold Apple businesses, I would likely still be pursuing my original idea of training one Gold Apple to go back to his job surrounded by people who didn't want to get better at customer service. In most cases, the poor solitary Gold Apple would be either fired or ignored, and positive change wouldn't occur as quickly as I had hoped. It was genius to get a small group of Gold Apples together in one location to really show what excellent customer service could accomplish. A great idea which I didn't think of."

"Whoa there Steve, wait just a minute," Ross interrupted. "That idea did come from you. If the six of us hadn't been exposed to your rules and philosophies, and also your original idea, we would never have tweaked it slightly to focus on businesses instead of individuals. Don't sell yourself short; the idea resulted from you, even if you didn't put the specifics into place."

Steve chuckled, looking at Aaron. "They are all so fiercely loyal to me," he said. "Plus they're excellent Gold Apples so they don't want me to feel bad."

Steve looked at Ross affectionately. "I know we all had a hand in it, Ross. Thank you for your kind words. For the story of the Platinum apple card, it's important that I convey to Aaron that one man is not an island. I think it's a strength of ours that, in today's cutthroat business world, we're a group of people who are able and willing to put ego aside and help each other all work towards a common goal." Ross nodded in agreement.

"So, getting back to the story," Steve continued. "I realized that there would be others who might come along that could not only see my vision, but also share it and join us to take the Gold Apples to even greater heights. Remember, my vision is not just to provide excellent customer service, it's to someday have everyone both giving, and getting, excellent customer service wherever they go."

Steve sipped his coffee. "If I think of department stores that give excellent customer service, I can only think of one or two. A business legendary for its customer service shouldn't be the exception, it should be the rule," Steve looked at Ross. "Is there room in this town for another restaurant that gives excellent customer service?" Ross nodded. "I think so too." Steve said. "But a second one isn't coming to mind, and I've been to most of them."

"Platinum apple cards," Steve continued, "are given to people that I feel have the ability and creativity to push the Gold Apples even further than we've been able to go so far. They are the new blood that can help us explode into success. A Platinum brings new perspectives and ideas, which are powerful. I think that you, Aaron, can propel us further than I could ever dream of going, and much faster than I could imagine doing it."

Steve paused to let the information sink in, while Aaron sat quietly, absorbing.

Finally Aaron spoke. "That's a pretty short way to introduce a very large topic."

"Not really." Steve said. "You've spent a few hours a week for the past few weeks getting to know the Gold Apples. You've learned our basic rules of customer service, how we formed into a group, what our goals are, and how we've moved towards the successes over the past few years. I've sent you to the best of us to get the clearest understanding, and I think you've understood it all very well. So this is just one little step, to share what we would like you to help us do."

"Let me ask you this question, Aaron." Steve leaned forward with interest. "Have you said to yourself over the past few weeks, "Well that sounds interesting, I bet if they just did this at Al's, or if they were to do something like this at Jake's, then they would be even more successful still?"

Aaron's grinned in reply.

"I thought so," Steve nodded. "I'm also guessing that when I presented my story about the challenges of growing the Gold Apple organization you had ideas that popped into your head for growing it even more."

Aaron nodded.

"Great!" Steve exclaimed. "That's the kind of thing I was expecting. You struck me as a guy who wants to be aggressive and grow something. You also have a masterful command of customer service. The Gold Apples movement needs to continue to grow. Like I've said before, we could find ten million Gold Apples and still have room for another 100 million more. We're at 820 identified and there are so many more still out there waiting to be found. Will you help us find them and help them to prosper?"

"How can you help them prosper?" Aaron asked.

"In whatever ways they define prosper. Some want to make more money, some want to help others. Some want to open their own business. Every one of them wants to enjoy their lives. Usually that involves doing something they are good at and something that they love to do, showing the world how powerful excellent customer service really is. We can also begin to have the Gold Apples monetarily compensated better for what they do. Undiscovered Gold Apples are underpaid and underappreciated. The 820 Gold Apples that we've discovered now make at least double the money they were making before we found them."

"You mean averaged out over the bunch?" Aaron questioned.

"No, I mean per individual." Steve said. "At this restaurant a Gold Apple dishwasher makes at least twice as much as a dishwasher at any restaurant in town, often more than that. The same is true for every Gold Apple business. We double the pay from the employee standard rate of that industry. Tips are also significantly larger. Great service gets tips even in jobs that don't traditionally receive them." Aaron nodded remembering tipping Dave at the gas station, a place he did not usually tip. "That doesn't even take into account the Gold Apples that go on to trade up for newer better jobs."

"Jake told you about the pit boss that was offered a high paying job with a Fortune 500 company right?" Aaron nodded remembering the story of the young man who went from a gas station wage to a six figure income training and teaching customer service. "Well that young man would almost certainly have remained a poor worker in the system of minimum wage jobs if he hadn't been given an outlet to shine in. His education and network of important contacts, until he joined the gas station, was very limited. He came from a family that couldn't afford to send him to university, which in today's work place is often an essential prerequisite to a decent income. But because he could provide excellent customer service and had a place to showcase his talents, he's now living better than he ever dreamed possible. I want to do that for not just a few hundred people, but for millions."

"That's a lofty goal, Steve," Aaron said appreciatively.

"If you're going spend the time and energy to make a goal," Steve said, "it might as well be a big one."

"I agree with you." Aaron said. "So what's next? Now that I know what you would like from me, how do I go about doing it?"

"The next step is that you come to work for me," Steve said. "I put you on my payroll, and over the next few months you get to know everything about the Gold Apples and the businesses that are involved. I expect that you'll come up with ideas on how to improve some of them. Together, you and I can discuss and implement them."

"Sounds interesting."

"Oh, it will be." Steve assured him. "Then, after a few months you might decide to start a Gold Apple business of your own. You've already indicated that you were ready to start your own business. I recall hearing that you expressed interest in a franchise of the some of the businesses you've already visited."

Aaron smiled.

"I'm hoping, however," Steve continued, "That you will think of a new business which will enable you to discover even more Gold Apples in less time than we have so far. If you come up with a business idea, I'll fund you to get it started. I ask to own a modest 10% of the business and will provide the cash and any other resources at my disposal to help you get it going."

Aaron was stunned to hear this. Angel investors were very difficult to find and they often wanted much more than 10% of a business. This was a very generous offer to receive from Steve, and Aaron said so now.

Steve smiled calmly. "My offer is generous to you, but selfish for the Gold Apples. I have a great feeling about you, Aaron, and I'm very confident that you can do remarkable things if given the opportunity. I'm happy to be in a position to give you the opportunity. So what do you say? Will you join us?

Aaron paused to think about Steve's offer, but it didn't take him long to accept.

# Chapter 12

"Steve is off the phone now, Aaron." Rebecca said, looking up from her desk. "Go in whenever you're ready."

Aaron stood up and walked towards the door. "Thanks Becca." he said, reaching for the handle.

Aaron gave Steve's office a quick glance as he entered, thinking how much more familiar it had become since first entering it six months ago.

During that time, Aaron had worked very closely with Steve, visiting all of the Gold Apple businesses and getting to know them all intimately. Each Gold Apple business was as spectacular as the three that he had first visited. Every single one claimed the top position in its market in both customer service and success. Aaron had been responsible for implementing exciting new strategies which had helped many of the businesses prosper even further. Steve and the business Gold Apples were extremely impressed with his knowledge of customer service, as well as his seemingly endless ideas on how to improve and grow. Aaron was also able to meet with some of the other Platinum Gold Apples. They were all as remarkably talented as Steve had claimed and Aaron was working with a few of them on some aggressive new projects.

Gold Apples continued to be discovered and cards given out. There was a new count of 1122 current Gold Apples, and some had even been discovered by Aaron! Steve's analogy of how a person breathes made it very easy to identify Gold Apples, and the rules of customer service had been witnessed in action so often by Aaron, that he saw clearly why they were good indicators of excellent customer service too.

The economy had taken a severe downturn shortly after Aaron had come on board, but the Gold Apple businesses were not concerned about this. They optimistically agreed that no matter what happened to the economy, people would always want great customer service and the products that the Gold Apple businesses offered. To prove that this was indeed true, the Gold Apple businesses were growing faster than ever. It was no surprise really: when people have less money to spend, they become more discerning about how they spend it. Many were clearly choosing to spend their money at places that gave great service. Steve had always maintained that great customer service was recession proof and, during this recession, the Gold Apple businesses were proving his statement to be 100% accurate.

New Gold Apple businesses were also brought on board or "into the orchard" as Steve liked to say. One platinum gold apple had come up with a new idea for finding and recruiting new businesses which had worked extremely well. The number of businesses had grown from 13 to 21 in just four months. This number impressed everyone and the responsible Platinum had turned the method and recruitment process into a business for herself. Many more businesses were expected to join.

During his time with the Gold Apples and Steve, Aaron had constantly been searching for a new business of his own to start. He'd been in no real rush since he was learning the ropes and contributing a great deal to the success of the whole group. An idea had finally occurred to him, and that's why he was here today: to pitch the business plan to Steve.

Steve was over by the bar, getting a mineral water for himself, and green tea for Aaron. He asked Aaron for a couple of quick updates on current projects they were working on together and, as Steve poured the tea, Aaron quickly brought him up to speed. Steve nodded and walked over to sit down on the couch, handing Aaron his drink.

"I've got an idea for a business." Aaron said with a smile.

"Excellent!" Steve beamed proudly. "I thought something might be up, the past few days you seemed preoccupied. I can't wait to hear about it. Are you ready to pitch it now?"

"Yeah," Aaron nodded. "I think so. I'm confident you will give me some advice which will make me need more time to fine tune it, but I'm ready to pitch it to you."

"Ok, that's great." Steve was completely interested. "Let me quickly shift into 'Business Destroyer' mode."

Aaron grinned. 'Business Destroyer' mode was Steve's name for when he ventured from his regular positive outlook into a more negative state of mind. Steve believed in seeing things from both sides of the fence, especially a new business. Too many businesses were formed with only the positive aspects considered. Steve was very good at identifying unforeseen negatives that could destroy a business before it even had the chance to get off the ground. General consensus among the Gold Apples was that if a pitch could still seem plausible after a session with the Business Destroyer, then odds were very good that the idea could succeed.

"Alright," Steve's regularly jovial face took on a stern appearance as he got into character. "Begin your weak pitch."

For the next two hours Aaron pitched his business idea to Steve. There were many intense questions followed by well-prepared answers. Aaron had put considerable thought into this new business and it was evident from his proposal to Steve. The business plan was excellent, including all of the information necessary for a shrewd investor like Steve to be able to make an educated appraisal.

After intensely scrutinizing the projections, forecasts, targeted customer base, and a plethora of other details, Aaron asked Steve for his opinion.

Steve sat silently considering the information. Apparently he had either run out of questions, or else he had enough info to make a judgment on Aaron's proposal. The two sat together in silence for some time, Steve considering what he had just heard from every angle, and Aaron patiently letting Steve work through his thoughts.

Finally, Steve nodded to himself and Aaron took the opportunity to ask for feed back. "Go ahead," Aaron invited, "tell me why it won't work."

Steve smiled. "Well it's definitely an aggressive and energetic idea. If you try this I'm not sure you'll have time to even sleep, you're going to be busy with all the hats that you're suggesting you wear. I think it can all work though. I hoped that you would have some great ideas for a good business, and you haven't disappointed me at all. I say let's go for it. I agree that even small success from your plan will be significantly more than we have done to date. Honestly, though, I think this will succeed way beyond any of our expectations."

"I'm glad you like the idea and want to go ahead with it." Aaron allowed himself to show his true excitement now that the pitch had been given, and accepted.

"I'll help as much you as much as you need me to." Steve offered. "I'm ready to get started as soon as you like."

"How about right now?" Aaron asked.

Steve smiled.

They got started.

**Afterword**

I'm hoping that you're curious about what happened next. Aaron's new business took off like a rocket just as Steve had hoped it would!

Gold Apples are a real group of people; you've likely even run into some of them whether they are official or still undiscovered members. That's one of the great things about Gold Apples, even if they haven't been handed the card yet, they'll still astound you by providing excellent customer service to everyone around them.

Can amazing customer service really be the key to a great and successful business? Excellent customer service alone will not make a great business will it?

The answer is a resounding yes!